COLLECTED WORKS OF
CHARLES H. SPURGEON

TW ALEXANDER
01/09

COLLECTED WORKS OF CHARLES H. SPURGEON

Early Religious Impressions
A Defense of Calvinism
Exposition: 1 John 3:1-10
Happy Childhood at Stambourne
The Kind of Revival We Need
The Great Change—Conversion
The Greatest Fight in the World
A Puritan Catechism
A Traveller's Letters Home

BIBLIOBAZAAR

COLLECTED WORKS OF
CHARLES H. SPURGEON

CONTENTS

EARLY RELIGIOUS IMPRESSIONS

MY FATHER AND MOTHER.

It would not be easy for some of us to recall the hour when we first heard the name of Jesus. In very infancy that sweet sound was as familiar to our ear as the hush of lullaby. Our earliest recollections are associated with the house of God, the family altar, the Holy Bible, the sacred song, and the fervent prayer. Like young Samuels, we were lighted to our rest by the lamps of the sanctuary, and were awakened by the sound of the morning hymn. Many a time has the man of God, whom a parent's hospitality has entertained, implored a blessing on our head, desiring in all sincerity that we might early call the Redeemer blessed; and to his petition a mother's earnest "Amen" has solemnly responded. Perhaps the first song we learned to sing was concerning the children's best Friend. The first book that we began to read contained His sweet name, and many were the times when we were pressed by godly ones to think of Jesus, and to give our young hearts to Him.—C. H. S.

* * * * *

I WAS privileged with godly parents, watched with jealous eyes, scarcely ever permitted to mingle with questionable associates, warned not to listen to anything profane or licentious, and taught the way of God from my youth up. There came a time when the solemnities of eternity pressed upon me for a decision, and when a mother's tears and a father's supplications were offered to Heaven on my behalf. At such a time, had I not been helped by the grace of God, but had I been left alone to do violence to conscience, and to struggle against conviction, I might perhaps have been at this moment dead, buried, and doomed, having through a course of vice brought myself to my grave, or I might have been as earnest a ringleader amongst the ungodly as I now desire to be an eager champion for Christ and His truth.

I do speak of myself with many deep regrets of heart. I hid as it were my face from Him, and I let the years run round,—not without twinges of conscience, not without rebukes, when I knew how much I needed a Saviour; not without the warnings which came from others whom I saw happy and rejoicing in Christ, while I had no share in His salvation. Still, I put it off, as others are doing, from day to day, and month to month, and thought that Christ might come in some odd hour, and when I had nothing else to do, I might think of Him whose blood could cleanse me. O my soul, I could fain smite thee now! Truly, I could lay this rod about my own heart to think that weeks and months should have rolled over my head, and I should have hid as it were my face from Christ in wilful neglect of my dear Lord whose heart had bled for me.

Children are often very reticent to their parents. Often and often have spoken I with young lads about their souls, and they have told me they could not talk to fathers upon such matters. I know it was so with me. When I was under concern of soul, the last persons I should have elected to speak to upon religion would been my parents,—not through want of love to them, nor absence of love on their part; but so it was. A strange feeling of diffidence pervades a seeking soul, and drives it from its friends. Yet I cannot tell how much I owe to the solemn words of my good mother. It was the custom, on Sunday evenings, while we were yet little children, for her to stay at home with us, and then we sat round the table, and read verse by verse, and she explained the Scripture to us. After that was done, then came the time of pleading; there was a little piece of Alleine's *Alarm*, or of Baxter's *Call to the Unconverted*, and this was read with pointed observations made to each of us as we sat round the table; and the question was asked, how long it would be before we would think about our state, how long before we would seek the Lord. Then came a mother's prayer, and some of the words of that prayer we shall never forget, even when our hair is grey. I remember, on one occasion, her praying thus: "Now, Lord, if my children go on in their sins, it will not be from ignorance that they perish, and my soul must bear a swift witness against them at the day of judgment if they lay not hold of Christ." That thought of a mother's bearing swift witness against me, pierced my conscience, and stirred my heart. When I was a child, if I had done anything wrong, I did not need anybody to tell me of it; I told myself of it, and I have cried myself to sleep many a time with the consciousness that I had done wrong; and when I came to know the Lord, I felt very grateful to Him because He had given me a tender conscience.

Fathers and mothers are the most natural agents for God to use in the salvation of their children. I am sure that, in my early youth, no teaching ever made such an impression upon my mind as the instruction of my mother; neither can I conceive that, to any child, there can be one who will have such influence over the heart as the mother who has so tenderly cared for her offspring. A man with a soul so dead as not to be moved by the sacred name of "mother" is creation's blot. Never could it be possible for any man to estimate what he owes to a godly mother. Certainly I have not the powers of speech with which to set forth my valuation of the choice blessing which the Lord bestowed on me in making me the son of one who prayed *for* me, and prayed *with* me. How can I ever forget her tearful eye when she warned me to escape from the wrath to come? I thought her lips right eloquent; others might not think so, but they certainly were eloquent to me. How can I ever forget when she bowed her knee, and with her arms about my neck, prayed, "Oh, that my son might live before Thee!" Nor can her frown be effaced from my memory,—that solemn, loving frown, when she rebuked my budding iniquities; and her smiles have never faded from my recollection,—the beaming of her countenance when she rejoiced to see some good thing in me towards the Lord God of Israel.

Well do I remember hearing my father speak of an incident that greatly impressed him. He used to be frequently away from home preaching, and at one time, as he was on his way to a service, he feared that he was neglecting his own family while caring for the souls of others. He therefore turned back, and went to his home. On arriving there, he was surprised to find no one in the lower rooms of the house; but, on ascending the stairs, he heard a sound as of someone engaged in prayer. On listening at the bedroom door, he discovered that it was my mother, pleading most earnestly for the salvation of all her children, and specially praying for Charles, her first-born and strong-willed son. My father felt that he might safely go about his Master's business while his dear wife was caring so well for the spiritual interests of the boys and girls at home, so he did not disturb her, but proceeded at once to fulfil his preaching engagement.

My mother said to me, one day, "Ah, Charles! I often prayed the Lord to make you a Christian, but I never asked that you might become a Baptist." I could not resist the temptation to reply, "Ah, mother ! the Lord has answered your prayer with His usual bounty, and given you exceeding abundantly above what you asked or thought."

Up to the age of fourteen, I had not even heard of people called Baptists; and when I did hear of them, it was not at all a favourable report that was given to me concerning them. I do not suppose my parents meant me to believe that Baptists were bad people; but I certainly did think so; and I cannot help feeling that, somewhere or other, I must have heard some calumnies against them, or else how should I have had that opinion?

I remember seeing a baby sprinkled within less than an hour of its death; and I seem to hear even now the comfort which a certain good man gave to the bereaved parents,—"What a mercy the child was baptized! What a consolation it must be!" This was in an Independent family, and the words were spoken by an Independent minister.

I knew an instance of an aged minister, of the same persuasion, who sprinkled a little boy, although the father was averse to it. The child was running about in the hall of the minister's house, and his mother was looking on. He was caught up, and the pious man exclaimed, "Come along, Mrs. S_____, the poor child shall not live like a heathen any longer." So the conjuration was performed, and the little boy was put into the Paedo-Baptist covenant. He was not only suffered to come, but forced to come; and, doubtless, went on his way rejoicing to think it was over.

It is said by some that children cannot understand the great mysteries of religion. We even know some Sunday-school teachers who cautiously avoid mentioning the great doctrines of the gospel, because they think the children are not prepared to receive them. Alas! the same mistake has crept into the pulpit; for it is currently believed, among a certain class of preachers, that many of the doctrines of the Word of God, although true, are not fit to be taught to the people, since they would pervert them to their own destruction. Away with such priestcraft! Whatever God has revealed ought to be preached. Whatever HE has revealed, if I am not capable of understanding it, I will still believe and preach it. I do hold that there is no doctrine of the Word of God which a child, if he be capable of salvation, is not capable of receiving. I would have children taught all the great doctrines of truth without a solitary exception, that they may in their after days hold fast by them.

I can bear witness that children can understand the Scriptures; for I am sure that, when but a child, I could have discussed many a knotty point of controversial theology, having heard both sides of the question freely stated among my father's circle of friends. In fact, children are capable of understanding some things in early life, which we hardly understand afterwards. Children have eminently a simplicity of faith, and simplicity of faith is akin to the highest knowledge; indeed, I know not that there is much distinction between the simplicity of a child and the genius of the profoundest mind. He who receives things simply, as a child, will often have ideas which the man who is prone to make a syllogism of everything will never attain unto. If you wish to know whether children can be taught, I point you to many in our churches, and in pious families,—not prodigies, but such as we frequently see,— Timothys and Samuels, and little girls, too, who have early come to know a Saviour's love. As soon as a child is capable of being lost, it is capable of being saved. As soon as a child can sin, that child can, if God's grace assist it, believe and receive the Word of God. As soon as children can learn evil, be assured that they are competent, under the teaching of the Holy Spirit, to learn good.

In the household in which I was trained, no cooking was ever done on the Sabbath; and if in the winter time something hot was brought on the table, it was a pudding prepared on the Saturday, or a few potatoes, which took but little trouble to warm. Is not this far better, far more Christian-like, than preparing a great Sunday feast, and compelling servants to slave in the kitchen? If the horse was taken out because the distance to the meeting-house was too great, or the weather too rough for walking, Christians of the good old school always gave the animal its Sabbath on the Saturday or the Monday; and as to the coachman, when they employed one, they always took care to give him time to put up the horse, that he might come in and worship with the family, and they were content to wait till he could come round for them after service, for they did not want him to lose even the Benediction.

Ought it not to be so everywhere? Our servants should be regarded as a part of the family, and we should study their comfort as well as our own, if for no other reason, certainly, because they will then study ours; but, above all, we should remember their souls, and give them every opportunity to enjoy the means of grace. How can they do this if we make the Lord's-day as much a work-day as any in the week? We are not of those who think it wicked to boil a kettle for tea on a Sunday, nor can we yield to the demands of some, that everybody, however feeble, or however distant his abode, should walk to the place of worship. To some, such a walk would be working with a vengeance, and to many an absolute deprivation of the means of grace; but, still, we must not allow unnecessary labour in or about our habitations on the Lord's-day, and must devise means to make the necessary work as light as-possible. Is a hot joint preferable to a servant's soul? Is it fair to keep a girl at home merely for our own needless gratification? Especially, is this justifiable in the case of those who fare sumptuously every day?

* * * * *

I recollect, when I was a boy, hearing a minister preach from this text, "Who can find a virtuous woman? for her price is far above rubies." The opening of that memorable discourse was somewhat in this fashion:—"'Who can find a virtuous woman?' Why, anyone who chooses to look for her; and the only reason why Solomon could not find her was because he looked in the wrong place. Virtuous women kept clear of a king who had such a multitude of wives. But," said the preacher, "if Solomon were here now, and were made truly wise, he would not long, ask,—'Who can find a virtuous woman?' He would join the church, and find himself at once among a band of holy women, whose adornment is a meek and quiet spirit. If he were permitted to look in upon the Dorcas meeting, he would see many of the sort of whom he once said, 'She stretcheth out her hand to the poor; yea, she reacheth forth her hands to the needy.' If he would adjourn to the Sunday-school, he would there meet with others of whom he would say, 'She openeth her mouth with wisdom; and in her tongue is the law of kindness.' We, who serve the Lord Jesus, meet many a time with virtuous women, of each of whom we could say with the wise king, 'Her price is far above rubies.'"

The preacher of whom I have spoken, interested me by the remark, "Why 'above *rubies*'? Why not above *diamonds*? My brethren, the diamond is but a pale and sickly stone, which needs the glare of candle-light or gas to set it off; but the ruby is a ruddy, healthy gem, which is beautiful by daylight. Lovely is the woman whose face is full of the glow of activity in domestic life. That is the kind of woman who makes the housewife in whom the heart of her husband safely trusteth."

Whatever one may think of the correctness of the exposition, the sentiment of the preacher was sound and practical.

I have not all pleasant reminiscences of the preachers of my boyhood. I used to hear a divine who had a habit, after he had uttered about a dozen sentences, of saying, "As I have already observed," or, "I repeat what I before remarked." Well, good soul, as there was nothing particular in what he had said, the repetition only revealed the more clearly the nakedness of the land. If it was very good, and, you said it forcibly, why go over it again? And if it was a feeble affair, why exhibit it a second time? Occasionally, of course, the repetition of a few sentences may be very telling; anything may be good occasionally, and yet be very vicious as a habit. Who wonders that people do not listen the first time when they know it is all to come over again? I once heard a most esteemed minister, who mumbled sadly, compared to "a humble bee in a pitcher,"—a vulgar metaphor, no doubt, but so exactly descriptive, that it brings to my mind the droning sound at this instant most distinctly, and reminds me of the parody upon Gray's *Elegy*:—

> "Now fades the glimmering subject from the sight,
>   And all the air a sleepy stillness holds,
> Save where the parson hums his droning flight,
> And drowsy tinklings lull the slumb'ring folds."

What a pity that a man who from his heart delivered doctrines of undoubted value, in language the most appropriate, should commit ministerial suicide by harping on one string, when the Lord had given him an instrument of many strings to play upon! Alas! alas! for that dreary voice, it hummed and hummed, like a mill-wheel, to the same unmusical tune, whether its owner spake of Heaven or hell, eternal life or everlasting wrath. It might be, by accident, a little louder or softer, according to the length of the sentence; but its tone was still the same, a dreary waste of sound, howling wilderness of speech in which there was no possible relief, no variety, no music, nothing but horrible sameness. When the wind blows through the Æolian harp, it swells through all the chords; but the Heavenly wind, passing through some men, spends itself upon one string, and that, for the most part, the most out of tune of the whole. Grace alone could enable hearers to edify under the drum—drum—drum of some divines. I think an impartial jury would bring in a verdict of justifiable slumbering in many cases where the sound emanating from the preacher lulls to sleep by its reiterated note.

I have a very lively, or rather a deadly, recollection of a certain series of discourses on the Hebrews, which made a deep impression on my mind of the most undesirable kind. I wished frequently that the Hebrews had kept the Epistle to themselves, for it sadly bored one poor Gentile lad. By the time the seventh or eighth discourse had been delivered, only the very good people could stand it: these, of course, declared that they never heard more valuable expositions, but to those of a more carnal judgment it appeared that each sermon increased in dulness. Paul, in that Epistle, exhorts us to *suffer* the word of exhortation, and we did so. I also recollect hearing in my younger days long passages out of Daniel, which might have been exceedingly instructive to me if I had obtained the remotest conception of what they meant. I remember hearing a sermon from these words, "Who passing through the valley of Baca make it a well." Certainly, the preacher did not make his sermon a well, for it was as dry as a stick, and not worth hearing. There was nothing like cheerfulness in it; but all the way through a flood of declamation against hopeful Christians, against people going to Heaven who are not always grumbling, and murmuring, and doubting; fumbling for their evidences amidst the exercises of their own hearts, ever reading and striving to rival Job and Jeremiah in grief, taking the Lamentations as the fit expression of their own lips, troubling their poor brains, and vexing their poor hearts, and smarting, and crying, and wearying themselves with the perpetual habit of complaining against God, saying, "My stroke is heavier than my groaning."

I used to hear a minister whose preaching was, as far as I could make it out, "Do this, and do that, and do the other, and you will be saved." According to his theory, to pray was a very easy thing; to make yourself a new heart, was a thing of a few instants, and could be done at almost any time; and I really thought that I could turn to Christ when I pleased, and that therefore I could put it off to the last part of my life, when it might be conveniently done upon a sick bed. But when the Lord gave my soul its first shakings in conviction, I soon knew better. I went to pray; I did pray, God knoweth, but it seemed to me that I did not. What, I approach the throne? Such a wretch as I lay hold on the promise? I venture to hope that God could look on me? It seemed impossible. A tear, a groan, and sometimes not so much as that, an "Ah!" a "Would that!" a "But,"—the lip could not utter more. It was prayer, but it did not seem so then. Oh, how hard is prevailing prayer to a poor God-provoking sinner! Where was the power to lay hold on God's strength, or wrestle with the angel? Certainly not in me, for I was weak as water, and sometimes hard as the nether millstone.

Once, under a powerful sermon, my heart shook within me, and was dissolved in the midst of my bowels; I thought I would seek the Lord, and I bowed my knee, and wrestled, and poured out my heart before Him. Again I ventured within His sanctuary to hear His Word, hoping that in some favoured hour He would send a precious promise to my consolation; but, ah! that wretched afternoon, I heard a sermon wherein Christ was not; I had no longer any hope. I would have sipped at that fountain, but I was driven away; I felt that I would have believed in Christ, and I longed and sighed for Him. But, ah! that dreadful sermon, and those terrible things that were uttered; my poor soul knew not what was truth, or what was error; but I thought the man was surely preaching the truth, and I was driven back. I dared not go, I could not believe, I could not lay hold on Christ; I was shut out, if no one else was.

A DEFENSE OF CALVINISM

"The old truth that Calvin preached, that Augustine preached, that Paul preached, is the truth that I must preach today, or else be false to my conscience and my God. I cannot shape the truth; I know of no such thing as paring off the rough edges of a doctrine. John Knox's gospel is my gospel. That which thundered through Scotland must thunder through England again."—C. H. Spurgeon

IT IS A GREAT THING to begin the Christian life by believing good solid doctrine. Some people have received twenty different "gospels" in as many years; how many more they will accept before they get to their journey's end, it would be difficult to predict. I thank God that He early taught me *the* gospel, and I have been so perfectly satisfied with it, that I do not want to know any other. Constant change of creed is sure loss. If a tree has to be taken up two or three times a year, you will not need to build a very large loft in which to store the apples. When people are always shifting their doctrinal principles, they are not likely to bring forth much fruit to the glory of God. It is good for young believers to begin with a firm hold upon those great fundamental doctrines which the Lord has taught in His Word. Why, if I believed what some preach about the temporary, trumpery salvation which only lasts for a time, I would scarcely be at all grateful for it; but when I know that those whom God saves He saves with an everlasting salvation, when I know that He gives to them an everlasting righteousness, when I know that He settles them on an everlasting foundation of everlasting love, and that He will bring them to His everlasting kingdom, oh, then I do wonder, and I am astonished that such a blessing as this should ever have been given to me!

"Pause, my soul! adore, and wonder!
Ask, 'Oh, why such love to me?'
Grace hath put me in the number
Of the Saviour's family:
Hallelujah!
Thanks, eternal thanks, to Thee!"

I suppose there are some persons whose minds naturally incline towards the doctrine of free-will. I can only say that mine inclines as naturally towards the doctrines of sovereign grace. Sometimes, when I see some of the worst characters in the street, I feel as if my heart must burst forth in tears of gratitude that God has never let me act as they have done! I have thought, if God had left me alone, and had not touched me by His grace, what a great sinner I should have been! I should have run to the utmost lengths of sin, dived into the very depths of evil, nor should I have stopped at any vice or folly, if God had not restrained me. I feel that I should have been a very king of sinners, if God had let me alone. I cannot understand the reason why I am saved, except upon the ground that God would have it so. I cannot, if I look ever so earnestly, discover any kind of reason in myself why I should be a partaker of Divine grace. If I am not at this moment without Christ, it is only because Christ Jesus would have His will with me, and that will was that I should be with Him where He is, and should share His glory. I can put the crown nowhere but upon the head of Him whose mighty grace has saved me from going down into the pit. Looking back on my past life, I can see that the dawning of it all was of God; of God effectively. I took no torch with which to light the sun, but the sun enlightened me. I did not commence my spiritual life—no, I rather kicked, and struggled against the things of the Spirit: when He drew me, for a time I did not run after Him: there was a natural hatred in my soul of everything holy and good. Wooings were lost upon me—warnings were cast to the wind—thunders were despised; and as for the whispers of His love, they were rejected as being less than nothing and vanity. But, sure I am, I can say now, speaking on behalf of myself, "He only is my salvation." It was He who turned my heart, and brought me down on my knees before Him. I can in very deed, say with Doddridge and Toplady—

> "Grace taught my soul to pray,
> And made my eyes o'erflow;"

and coming to this moment, I can add—

> "'Tis grace *has* kept me to this day,
> And will not let me go."

Well can I remember the manner in which I learned the doctrines of grace in a single instant. Born, as all of us are by nature, an Arminian, I still believed the old things I had heard continually from the pulpit, and did not see the grace of God. When I was coming to Christ, I thought I was doing it all myself, and though I sought the Lord earnestly, I had no idea the Lord was seeking me. I do not think the young convert is at first aware of this. I can recall the very day and hour when first I received those truths in my own soul—when they were, as John Bunyan says, burnt into my heart as with a hot iron, and I can recollect how I felt that I had grown on a sudden from a babe into a man—that I had made progress in Scriptural knowledge, through having found, once for all, the clue to the truth of God. One week-night, when I was sitting in the house of God, I was not thinking much about the preacher's sermon, for I did not believe it. The thought struck me, *How did you come to be a Christian?* I sought the Lord. *But how did you come to seek the Lord?* The truth flashed across my mind in a moment—I should not have sought Him unless there had been some previous influence in my mind to *make me* seek Him. I prayed, thought I, but then I asked myself, *How came I to pray?* I was induced to pray by reading the Scriptures. *How came I to read the Scriptures?* I did read them, but what led me to do so? Then, in a moment, I saw that God was at the bottom of it all, and that He was the Author of my faith, and so the whole doctrine of grace opened up to me, and from that doctrine I have not departed to this day, and I desire to make this my constant confession, "I ascribe my change wholly to God."

I once attended a service where the text happened to be, *"He* shall choose our inheritance for us;" and the good man who occupied the pulpit was more than a little of an Arminian. Therefore, when he commenced, he said, "This passage refers entirely to our temporal inheritance, it has nothing whatever to do with our everlasting destiny, for," said he, "we do not want Christ to choose for us in the matter of Heaven or hell. It is so plain and easy, that every man who has a grain of common sense will choose Heaven, and any person would know better than to choose hell. We have no need of any superior intelligence, or any greater Being, to choose Heaven or hell for us. It is left to our own free-will, and we have enough wisdom given us, sufficiently correct means to judge for ourselves," and therefore, as he very logically inferred, there was no necessity for Jesus Christ, or anyone, to make a choice for us. We could choose the inheritance for ourselves without any assistance. "Ah!" I thought, "but, my good brother, it may be very true that we *could*, but I think we should want something more than common sense before we *should* choose aright."

First, let me ask, must we not all of us admit an over-ruling Providence, and the appointment of Jehovah's hand, as to the means whereby we came into this world? Those men who think that, afterwards, we are left to our own free-will to choose this one or the other to direct our steps, must admit that our entrance into the world was not of our own will, but that God had then to choose for us. What circumstances were those in our power which led us to elect certain persons to be our parents? Had we anything to do with it? Did not God Himself appoint our parents, native place, and friends? Could He not have caused me to be born with the skin of the Hottentot, brought forth by a filthy mother who would nurse me in her "kraal," and teach me to bow down to Pagan gods, quite as easily as to have given me a pious mother, who would each morning and night bend her knee in prayer on my behalf? Or, might He not, if He had pleased, have given me some profligate to have been my parent, from whose lips I might have early heard fearful, filthy, and obscene language? Might He not have placed me where I should have had a drunken father, who would have immured me in a very dungeon of ignorance, and brought me up in the chains of crime? Was it not God's Providence that I had so happy a lot, that both my parents were His children, and endeavoured to train me up in the fear of the Lord?

John Newton used to tell a whimsical story, and laugh at it, too, of a good woman who said, in order to prove the doctrine of election, "Ah! sir, the Lord must have loved me before I was born, or else He would not have seen anything in me to love afterwards."

I am sure it is true in my case; I believe the doctrine of election, because I am quite certain that, if God had not chosen me, I should never have chosen Him; and I am sure He chose me before I was born, or else He never would have chosen me afterwards; and He must have elected me for reasons unknown to me, for I never could find any reason in myself why He should have looked upon me with special love. So I am forced to accept that great Biblical doctrine. I recollect an Arminian brother telling me that he had read the Scriptures through a score or more times, and could never find the doctrine of election in them. He added that he was sure he would have done so if it had been there, for he read the Word on his knees. I said to him, "I think you read the Bible in a very uncomfortable posture, and if you had read it in your easy chair, you would have been more likely to understand it. Pray, by all means, and the more, the better, but it is a piece of superstition to think there is anything in the posture in which a man puts himself for reading: and as to reading through the Bible twenty times without having found anything about the doctrine of election, the wonder is that you found anything at all: you must have galloped through it at such a rate that you were not likely to have any intelligible idea of the meaning of the Scriptures."

If it would be marvelous to see one river leap up from the earth full-grown, what would it be to gaze upon a vast spring from which all the rivers of the earth should at once come bubbling up, a million of them born at a birth? What a vision would it be! Who can conceive it. And yet the love of God is that fountain, from which all the rivers of mercy, which have ever gladdened our race—all the rivers of grace in time, and of glory hereafter—take their rise. My soul, stand thou at that sacred fountain-head, and adore and magnify, for ever and ever, God, even our Father, who hath loved us! In the very beginning, when this great universe lay in the mind of God, like unborn forests in the acorn cup; long ere the echoes awoke the solitudes; before the mountains were brought forth; and long ere the light flashed through the sky, God loved His chosen creatures. Before there was any created being—when the ether was not fanned by an angel's wing, when space itself had not an existence, when there was nothing save God alone—even then, in that loneliness of Deity, and in that deep quiet and profundity, His bowels moved with love for His chosen. Their names were written on His heart, and then were they dear to His soul. Jesus loved His people before the foundation of the world—even from eternity! and when He called me by His grace, He said to me, "I have loved *thee* with an everlasting love: therefore with lovingkindness have I drawn thee."

Then, in the fulness of time, He purchased me with His blood; He let His heart run out in one deep gaping wound for me long ere I loved Him. Yea, when He first came to me, did I not spurn Him? When He knocked at the door, and asked for entrance, did I not drive Him away, and do despite to His grace? Ah, I can remember that I full often did so until, at last, by the power of His effectual grace, He said, "I must, I will come in;" and then He turned my heart, and made me love Him. But even till now I should have resisted Him, had it not been for His grace. Well, then since He purchased me when I was dead in sins, does it not follow, as a consequence necessary and logical, that He must have loved me first? Did my Saviour die for me because I believed on Him? No; I was not then in existence; I had then no being. Could the Saviour, therefore, have died because I had faith, when I myself was not yet born? Could that have been possible? Could that have been the origin of the Saviour's love towards me? Oh! no; my Saviour died for me long before I believed. "But," says someone, "He foresaw that you would have faith; and, therefore, He loved you." What did He foresee about my faith? Did He foresee that I should get that faith myself, and that I should believe on Him of myself? No; Christ could not foresee that, because no Christian man will ever say that faith came of itself without the gift and without the working of the Holy Spirit. I have met with a great many believers, and talked with them about this matter; but I never knew one who could put his hand on his heart, and say, "I believed in Jesus without the assistance of the Holy Spirit."

I am bound to the doctrine of the depravity of the human heart, because I find myself depraved in heart, and have daily proofs that in my flesh there dwelleth no good thing. If God enters into covenant with unfallen man, man is so insignificant a creature that it must be an act of gracious condescension on the Lord's part; but if God enters into covenant with *sinful* man, he is then so offensive a creature that it must be, on God's part, an act of pure, free, rich, sovereign grace. When the Lord entered into covenant with me, I am sure that it was all of grace, nothing else but grace. When I remember what a den of unclean beasts and birds my heart was, and how strong was my unrenewed will, how obstinate and rebellious against the sovereignty of the Divine rule, I always feel inclined to take the very lowest room in my Father's house, and when I enter Heaven, it will be to go among the less than the least of all saints, and with the chief of sinners.

The late lamented Mr. Denham has put, at the foot of his portrait, a most admirable text, "Salvation is of the Lord." That is just an epitome of Calvinism; it is the sum and substance of it. If anyone should ask me what I mean by a Calvinist, I should reply, "He is one who says, *Salvation is of the Lord*." I cannot find in Scripture any other doctrine than this. It is the essence of the Bible. "He *only* is my rock and my salvation." Tell me anything contrary to this truth, and it will be a heresy; tell me a heresy, and I shall find its essence here, that it has departed from this great, this fundamental, this rock-truth, "God is my rock and my salvation." What is the heresy of Rome, but the addition of something to the perfect merits of Jesus Christ—the bringing in of the works of the flesh, to assist in our justification? And what is the heresy of Arminianism but the addition of something to the work of the Redeemer? Every heresy, if brought to the touchstone, will discover itself here. I have my own private opinion that there is no such thing as preaching Christ and Him crucified, unless we preach what nowadays is called Calvinism. It is a nickname to call it Calvinism; Calvinism is the gospel, and nothing else. I do not believe we can preach the gospel, if we do not preach justification by faith, without works; nor unless we preach the sovereignty of God in His dispensation of grace; nor unless we exalt the electing, unchangeable, eternal, immutable, conquering love of Jehovah; nor do I think we can preach the gospel, unless we base it upon the special and particular redemption of His elect and chosen people which Christ wrought out upon the cross; nor can I comprehend a gospel which lets saints fall away after they are called, and suffers the children of God to be burned in the fires of damnation after having once believed in Jesus. Such a gospel I abhor.

> "If ever it should come to pass,
> That sheep of Christ might fall away,
> My fickle, feeble soul, alas!
> Would fall a thousand times a day."

If one dear saint of God had perished, so might all; if one of the covenant ones be lost, so may all be; and then there is no gospel promise true, but the Bible is a lie, and there is nothing in it worth my acceptance. I will be an infidel at once when I can believe that a saint of God can ever fall finally. If God hath loved me once, then He will love me for ever. God has a master-mind; He arranged everything in His gigantic intellect long before He did it; and once having settled it, He never alters it, "This shall be done," saith He, and the iron hand of destiny marks it down, and it is brought to pass. "This is My purpose," and it stands, nor can earth or hell alter it. "This is My decree," saith He, "promulgate it, ye holy angels; rend it down from the gate of Heaven, ye devils, if ye can; but ye cannot alter the decree, it shall stand for ever." God altereth not His plans; why should He? He is Almighty, and therefore can perform His pleasure. Why should He? He is the All-wise, and therefore cannot have planned wrongly. Why should He? He is the everlasting God, and therefore cannot die before His plan is accomplished. Why should He change? Ye worthless atoms of earth, ephemera of a day, ye creeping insects upon this bay-leaf of existence, ye may change *your* plans, but He shall never, never change *His*. Has He told me that His plan is to save me? If so, I am for ever safe.

> "My name from the palms of His hands
> Eternity will not erase;
> Impress'd on His heart it remains,
> In marks of indelible grace."

I do not know how some people, who believe that a Christian can fall from grace, manage to be happy. It must be a very commendable thing in them to be able to get through a day without despair. If I did not believe the doctrine of the final perseverance of the saints, I think I should be of all men the most miserable, because I should lack any ground of comfort. I could not say, whatever state of heart I came into, that I should be like a well-spring of water, whose stream fails not; I should rather have to take the comparison of an intermittent spring, that might stop on a sudden, or a reservoir, which I had no reason to expect would always be full. I believe that the happiest of Christians and the truest of Christians are those who never dare to doubt God, but who take His Word simply as it stands, and believe it, and ask no questions, just feeling assured that if God has said it, it will be so. I bear my willing testimony that I have no reason, nor even the shadow of a reason, to doubt my Lord, and I challenge Heaven, and earth, and hell, to bring any proof that God is untrue. From the depths of hell I call the fiends, and from this earth I call the tried and afflicted believers, and to Heaven I appeal, and challenge the long experience of the blood-washed host, and there is not to be found in the three realms a single person who can bear witness to one fact which can disprove the faithfulness of God, or weaken His claim to be trusted by His servants. There are many things that may or may not happen, but this I know *shall* happen—

> "He *shall* present my soul,
> Unblemish'd and complete,
> Before the glory of His face,
> With joys divinely great."

All the purposes of man have been defeated, but not the purposes of God. The promises of man may be broken—many of them are made to be broken—but the promises of God shall all be fulfilled. He is a promise-maker, but He never was a promise-breaker; He is a promise-keeping God, and every one of His people shall prove it to be so. This is my grateful, personal confidence, "The Lord *will* perfect that which concerneth *me*"—unworthy *me*, lost and ruined *me*. He will yet save me; and—

> "I, among the blood-wash'd throng,
> Shall wave the palm, and wear the crown,
> And shout loud victory."

I go to a land which the plough of earth hath never upturned, where it is greener than earth's best pastures, and richer than her most abundant harvests ever saw. I go to a building of more gorgeous architecture than man hath ever builded; it is not of mortal design; it is "a building of God, a house not made with hands, eternal in the Heavens." All I shall know and enjoy in Heaven, will be given to me by the Lord, and I shall say, when at last I appear before Him—

> "Grace all the work shall crown
> Through everlasting days;
> It lays in Heaven the topmost stone,
> And well deserves the praise."

I know there are some who think it necessary to their system of theology to limit the merit of the blood of Jesus: if my theological system needed such a limitation, I would cast it to the winds. I cannot, I dare not allow the thought to find a lodging in my mind, it seems so near akin to blasphemy. In Christ's finished work I see an ocean of merit; my plummet finds no bottom, my eye discovers no shore. There must be sufficient efficacy in the blood of Christ, if God had so willed it, to have saved not only all in this world, but all in ten thousand worlds, had they transgressed their Maker's law. Once admit infinity into the matter, and limit is out of the question. Having a Divine Person for an offering, it is not consistent to conceive of limited value; bound and measure are terms inapplicable to the Divine sacrifice. The intent of the Divine purpose fixes the *application* of the infinite offering, but does not change it into a finite work. Think of the numbers upon whom God has bestowed His grace already. Think of the countless hosts in Heaven: if thou wert introduced there today, thou wouldst find it as easy to tell the stars, or the sands of the sea, as to count the multitudes that are before the throne even now. They have come from the East, and from the West, from the North, and from the South, and they are sitting down with Abraham, and with Isaac, and with Jacob in the Kingdom of God; and beside those in Heaven, think of the saved ones on earth. Blessed be God, His elect on earth are to be counted by millions, I believe, and the days are coming, brighter days than these, when there shall be multitudes upon multitudes brought to know the Saviour, and to rejoice in Him. The Father's love is not for a few only, but for an exceeding great company. "A great multitude, which no man could number," will be found in Heaven. A man can reckon up to very high figures; set to work your Newtons, your mightiest calculators, and they can count great numbers, but God and God alone can tell the multitude of His redeemed. I believe there will be more in Heaven than in hell. If anyone asks me why I think so, I answer, because Christ, in everything, is to "have the pre-eminence," and I cannot conceive how He could have the pre-eminence if there are to be more in the dominions of Satan than in Paradise. Moreover, I have never read that there is to be in hell a great multitude, which no man could number. I rejoice to know that the souls of all infants, as soon as they die, speed their way to Paradise. Think what a multitude there is of them! Then there are already in Heaven unnumbered myriads of the spirits of just men made perfect—the redeemed of all nations, and kindreds, and people, and tongues up till now; and there are better times coming, when the religion of Christ shall be universal; when—

> "He shall reign from pole to pole,
> With illimitable sway;"

when whole kingdoms shall bow down before Him, and nations shall be born in a day, and in the thousand years of the great millennial state there will be enough saved to make up all the deficiencies of the thousands of years that have gone before. Christ shall be Master everywhere, and His praise shall be sounded in every land. Christ shall have the pre-eminence at last; His train shall be far larger than that which shall attend the chariot of the grim monarch of hell.

Some persons love the doctrine of universal atonement because they say, "It is so beautiful. It is a lovely idea that Christ should have died for all men; it commends itself," they say, "to the instincts of humanity; there is something in it full of joy and beauty." I admit there is, but beauty may be often associated with falsehood. There is much which I might admire in the theory of universal redemption, but I will just show what the supposition necessarily involves. If Christ on His cross intended to save every man, then He intended to save those who were lost before He died. If the doctrine be true, that He died for all men, then He died for some who were in hell before He came into this world, for doubtless there were even then myriads there who had been cast away because of their sins. Once again, if it was Christ's intention to save all men, how deplorably has He been disappointed, for we have His own testimony that there is a lake which burneth with fire and brimstone, and into that pit of woe have been cast some of the very persons who, according to the theory of universal redemption, were bought with His blood. That seems to me a conception a thousand times more repulsive than any of those consequences which are said to be associated with the Calvinistic and Christian doctrine of special and particular redemption. To think that my Saviour died for men who were or are in hell, seems a supposition too horrible for me to entertain. To imagine for a moment that He was the Substitute for all the sons of men, and that God, having first punished the Substitute, afterwards punished the sinners themselves, seems to conflict with all my ideas of Divine justice. That Christ should offer an atonement and satisfaction for the sins of all men, and that afterwards some of those very men should be punished for the sins for which Christ had already atoned, appears to me to be the most monstrous iniquity that could ever have been imputed to Saturn, to Janus, to the goddess of the Thugs, or to the most diabolical heathen deities. God forbid that we should ever think thus of Jehovah, the just and wise and good!

There is no soul living who holds more firmly to the doctrines of grace than I do, and if any man asks me whether I am ashamed to be called a Calvinist, I answer—I wish to be called nothing but a Christian; but if you ask me, do I hold the doctrinal views which were held by John Calvin, I reply, I do in the main hold them, and rejoice to avow it. But far be it from me even to imagine that Zion contains none but Calvinistic Christians within her walls, or that there are none saved who do not hold our views. Most atrocious things have been spoken about the character and spiritual condition of John Wesley, the modern prince of Arminians. I can only say concerning him that, while I detest many of the doctrines which he preached, yet for the man himself I have a reverence second to no Wesleyan; and if there were wanted two apostles to be added to the number of the twelve, I do not believe that there could be found two men more fit to be so added than George Whitefield and John Wesley. The character of John Wesley stands beyond all imputation for self-sacrifice, zeal, holiness, and communion with God; he lived far above the ordinary level of common Christians, and was one "of whom the world was not worthy." I believe there are multitudes of men who cannot see these truths, or, at least, cannot see them in the way in which we put them, who nevertheless have received

Christ as their Saviour, and are as dear to the heart of the God of grace as the soundest Calvinist in or out of Heaven.

I do not think I differ from any of my Hyper-Calvinistic brethren in what I do believe, but I differ from them in what they do not believe. I do not hold any less than they do, but I hold a little more, and, I think, a little more of the truth revealed in the Scriptures. Not only are there a few cardinal doctrines, by which we can steer our ship North, South, East, or West, but as we study the Word, we shall begin to learn something about the North-west and North-east, and all else that lies between the four cardinal points. The system of truth revealed in the Scriptures is not simply one straight line, but two; and no man will ever get a right view of the gospel until he knows how to look at the two lines at once. For instance, I read in one Book of the Bible, "The Spirit and the bride say, Come. And let him that heareth say, Come. And let him that is athirst come. And whosoever will, let him take the water of life freely." Yet I am taught, in another part of the same inspired Word, that "it is not of him that willeth, nor of him that runneth, but of God that sheweth mercy." I see, in one place, God in providence presiding over all, and yet I see, and I cannot help seeing, that man acts as he pleases, and that God has left his actions, in a great measure, to his own free-will. Now, if I were to declare that man was so free to act that there was no control of God over his actions, I should be driven very near to atheism; and if, on the other hand, I should declare that God so over-rules all things that man is not free enough to be responsible, I should be driven at once into Antinomianism or fatalism. That God predestines, and yet that man is responsible, are two facts that few can see clearly. They are believed to be inconsistent and contradictory to each other. If, then, I find taught in one part of the Bible that everything is fore-ordained, *that is true*; and if I find, in another Scripture, that man is responsible for all his actions, *that is true*; and it is only my folly that leads me to imagine that these two truths can ever contradict each other. I do not believe they can ever be welded into one upon any earthly anvil, but they certainly shall be one in eternity. They are two lines that are so nearly parallel, that the human mind which pursues them farthest will never discover that they converge, but they do converge, and they will meet somewhere in eternity, close to the throne of God, whence all truth doth spring.

It is often said that the doctrines we believe have a tendency to lead us to sin. I have heard it asserted most positively, that those high doctrines which we love, and which we find in the Scriptures, are licentious ones. I do not know who will have the hardihood to make that assertion, when they consider that the holiest of men have been believers in them. I ask the man who dares to say that Calvinism is a licentious religion, what he thinks of the character of Augustine, or Calvin, or Whitefield, who in successive ages were the great exponents of the system of grace; or what will he say of the Puritans, whose works are full of them? Had a man been an Arminian in those days, he would have been accounted the vilest heretic breathing, but now *we* are looked upon as the heretics, and they as the orthodox. *We* have gone back to the old school; *we* can trace our descent from the apostles. It is that vein of free-grace, running through the sermonizing of Baptists, which has saved us as a denomination. Were it not for that, we should not stand where we are today. We can run a golden line up to Jesus Christ Himself, through a holy succession of mighty fathers, who all held these glorious truths; and we can ask concerning them, "Where will you find holier and better men in the world?" No doctrine is so calculated to preserve a man from sin as the doctrine of the grace of God. Those who have called it "a licentious doctrine" did not know anything at all about it. Poor ignorant things, they little knew that their own vile stuff was the most licentious doctrine under Heaven. If they knew the grace of God in truth, they would soon see that there was no preservative from lying like a knowledge that we are elect of God from the foundation of the world. There is nothing like a belief in my eternal perseverance, and the immutability of my Father's affection, which can keep me near to Him from a motive of simple gratitude. Nothing makes a man so virtuous as belief of the truth. A lying doctrine will soon beget a lying practice. A man cannot have an erroneous belief without by-and-by having an erroneous life. I believe the one thing naturally begets the other. Of all men, those have the most disinterested piety, the sublimest reverence, the most ardent devotion, who believe that they are saved by grace, without works, through faith, and that not of themselves, it is the gift of God. Christians should take heed, and see that it always is so, lest by any means Christ should be crucified afresh, and put to an open shame.

EXPOSITION: 1 JOHN 3:1-10

"Behold, what manner of love the Father hath bestowed upon us, that we should be called the sons of God: therefore the world knoweth us not, because it knew him not.

"Beloved, now are we the sons of God, and it doth not yet appear what we shall be: but we know that, when he shall appear, we shall be like him, for we shall see him as he is."

As dear Dr. Hawker said concerning this, there is a chapter in every word and a sermon in every letter. How it opens with a "Behold!" because it is such a striking portion of sacred Scripture, that the Holy Ghost would have us pay particular attention to it. "*Behold!*" says he, "read other Scriptures if you like, with a glance, but stop here. I have put up a way-mark to tell you there is something eminently worthy of attention buried beneath these words." "Behold, what manner of love the Father hath bestowed on *us.*" Consider who we were, and who we are now; ay, and what we feel ourselves to be even when divine grace is powerful in us. And yet, beloved, we are called "*the sons of God.*" It is said that when one of the learned heathens was translating this, he stopped and said, "No; it cannot be; let it be written 'Subjects,' not 'Sons,' for it is impossible we should called 'the sons of God.' "What a high relationship is that of a son to his father! What privileges a son has from his father! What liberties a son may take with his father! and oh! what obedience the son owes to his father, and what love the father feels towards the son! But all *that*, and more than *that*, we now have through Christ. "Behold!" ye angels! stop, ye seraphs! here is a thing more wonderful than heaven with its walls of jasper. Behold, universe! open thine eyes, O world. "Behold, what manner of love the Father hath bestowed upon us, that we should be called the sons of God; therefore the world knoweth us not, because it knew him not." Well, we are content to go with him in his humiliation, for we are to be exalted with him.

"*Beloved, now are we the sons of God.*" That is easy to read; but it is not so easy to feel. "*Now* are we the sons of God." How is it with your heart this morning? Are you in the lowest depths of sorrow and suffering? "*Now are you* a son of God." Does corruption rise within your spirit, and grace seem like a poor spark trampled under foot? "Beloved, *now* are *you* a son of God." Does your faith almost fail you? and are your graces like a candle well nigh blown out by the wind! Fear not, beloved; it is not your graces, it is not your frames, it is not your feelings, on which you are to live: you must live simply by naked faith on Christ. "Beloved, *now* are we the sons of God." With all these things against us, with the foot of the devil on our neck, and the sword in his hand ready to slay us—beloved *now* in the very depths of our sorrow, wherever we may be—*now*, as much in the valley as on the mountain, as much in the dungeon as in the palace, as much when broken on the wheel of suffering as when exalted on the wings of triumph—"beloved, *now* are we the sons of God." "Ah!" but you say, "see how I am arrayed! my graces are not bright; my righteousness does not shine with apparent glory." But read the next: "*It doth not yet appear what we shall be; but we know that when he shall appear, we shall be like him.*" We are not so much like him now, but we have some more refining process to undergo, and death itself, that best of all friends, is yet to wash us clean. "We know that when he shall appear, we shall be like him; for we shall see him as he is."

"*And every man that hath this hope in him, purifieth himself, even as he is pure.*

"*Whosoever committeth sin transgresseth also the law for sin is the transgression of the law.*

"*And ye know that he was manifested to take away our sins; and in him is no sin.*"

Believer, read these words in two senses. He was manifested to take away thy sins that thou hast committed; and that he accomplished, when "the just for the unjust," he sustained the penalties of them. And he was manifested to take away the power of thy sins; that is to say, to conquer thy reigning lusts, to take away thine evil imaginations, to purify thee, and make thee like himself. Well, beloved, what a mercy it is that some one was manifested to take away our sins from us! for some of us have been striving a long, long while, to conquer our sins, and we cannot do it. We thought we had driven them out, but they had "chariots of iron," and we could not overcome them; they lived "in the hill country," and we could not get near them. As often as we worsted them in one battle, they came upon us thick and strong, like an army of locusts; when heaps and heaps had been destroyed they seemed as thick as ever. Ah! but there is a thought—they shall all be taken away. "Ye know that he was manifested to take away our sins;" and so he will. The time will come when you and I shall stand without spot or blemish before the throne of God: for they are "without fault before the throne of God" at this moment, and so shall we be ere long.

"Whosoever abideth in him sinneth not: whosoever sinneth hath not seen him, neither known him."

This plain, simple verse, has been twisted by some who believe in the doctrine of perfection, and they have made it declare that it is possible for some to abide in Christ, and therefore not to sin. But you will remark that it does not say, that *some* that abide in Christ do not sin; but it says that *none* who abide in Christ sin. "*Whosoever* abideth in him sinneth not." Therefore this passage is not to be applied to a few who attain to what is called by our Arminian friends the fourth degree—perfection; but it appertains to all believers; and of every soul in Christ it may be said, that he sinneth not. In reading the Bible, we read it simply as we would read another book. We ought not to read it as a preacher his text, with the intention of making something out of every word; but we should read it as we find it written: "Whosoever abideth in Christ sinneth not." Now we are sure that cannot mean that he does not sin at all, but it means that sins not habitually, he sins not designedly, he sins not finally, so as to perish. The Bible often calls a man righteous; but that does not mean that he is perfectly righteous. It calls a man a sinner, but it does not imply that he may not have done some good deeds in his life; it means that that is the man's general character. So with the man who abides in Christ: his general character is not that he is a sinner, but that he is a saint—he sinneth not openly wilfully before men. In his own heart, he has much to confess, but his life before his fellow creatures is such a one that it can be said of him: "Whosoever abideth in him sinneth not; but whosoever sinneth [the sins of this world, in which the multitude indulge] hath not seen him, neither known him."

"*Little children, let no man deceive you: he that doeth righteousness is righteous, even as he is righteous.*"

That is the sign of it. Works are the fruits of grace. "He is righteous,"—not in himself; for mark how graces come in here— "He is righteous, even as HE is righteous." It will not allow our righteousness to be our own, but it brings us to Christ again. "He that doeth righteousness is righteous," not according to his own works, but "even as HE is righteous." Good works prove that I have perfect righteousness in Christ; they do not help the righteousness of Christ, nor yet in any way make me righteous. Good works are of no use whatever in the matter of justification: they only use they are, is, that they are for our comfort, for the benefit of others, and for the glory of God. "He that doeth righteousness is righteous, even as he is righteous. He that committeth sin is of the devil."

"*He that committeth sin is of the devil; for the devil sinneth from the beginning. For this purpose the Son of God was manifested, that he might destroy the works of the devil.*

"*Whosoever is born of God doth not commit sin; for his seed remaineth in him: and he cannot sin, because he is born of God.*

"*In this the children of God are manifest, and the children of the devil; whosoever doeth not righteousness is not of God, neither he that loveth not his brother.*"

It were well if we always remembered that practical godliness is the soul of godliness; that it is not talking religion, but walking religion which proves a man to be sincere; it is not having a religious tongue, but a religious heart; it is not a religious mouth, but a religious foot. The best evidence is the salvation of the soul. Avaunt! talkative; go thy way, thou mere professing formalist! Your ways lead down to hell, and your end shall be destruction; for "He that doeth righteousness is righteous, even as he is righteous. He that committeth sin is of the devil; for the devil sinneth from the beginning. For this purpose the Son of God was manifested, that he mighty destroy the works of the devil."

HAPPY CHILDHOOD AT STAMBOURNE

THE OLD MANSE AND MEETING-HOUSE,
STAMBOURNE.

Oh, the old house at home! who does not love it, the place of our childhood, the old roof-tree, the old cottage? There is no other village in all the world half so good as that particular village! True, the gates, and styles, and posts have been altered; but, still, there is an attachment to those old houses, the old tree in the park, and the old ivy-mantled tower. It is not very picturesque, perhaps, but we love to go to see it. We like to see the haunts of our boyhood. There is something pleasant in those old stairs where the clock used to stand; and in the room where grandmother was wont to bend her knee, and where we had family prayer. There is no place like that house after all.—C. H. S.

* * * * *

THIS drawing of the old Manse at Stambourne has far more charms for me than for any of my readers; but I hope that their generous kindness to the writer will cause them to be interested in it. Here my venerable grandfather lived for more than fifty years, and reared his rather numerous family. In its earlier days it must have been a very remarkable abode for a dissenting teacher; a clear evidence that either he had an estate of his own, or that those about him had large hearts and pockets. It was in all respects a gentleman's mansion of the olden times. The house has been supplanted by one which, I doubt not, is most acceptable to the excellent minister who occupies it; but to me it can never be one-half so dear as the revered old home in which I spent some of my earliest years. It is true the old parsonage had developed devotional tendencies, and seemed inclined to prostrate its venerable form, and therefore it might have fallen down of itself if it had not been removed by the builder; but, somehow, I wish it had kept up for ever and ever. I could have cried, "Builders, spare that home. Touch not a single tile, or bit of plaster;" but its hour was come, and so the earthly house was happily dissolved, to be succeeded by a more enduring fabric. The new house, as Smith told me, was "built on the same destruction." It stood near the chapel, so that the pastor was close to his work.

It looks a very noble parsonage, with its eight windows in front; but at least three, and I think four, of these were plastered up, and painted black, and then marked out in lines to imitate glass. They were not such very bad counterfeits, or the photograph would betray this. Some of us can remember the window tax, which seemed to regard light as a Latin commodity—*lux*, and therefore a luxury, and as such to be taxed. So much was paid on each aperture for the admission of light; but the minister's small income forced economy upon him, and so room after room of the manse was left in darkness, to be regarded by my childish mind with reverent awe. Over other windows were put up boards marked DAIRY, or CHEESE-ROOM, because by being labelled with these names they would escape the tribute. What a queer mind must his have been who first invented taxing the light of the sun! It was, no doubt, meant to be a fair way of estimating the size of a house, and thus getting at the wealth of the inhabitant; but, incidentally, it led occupiers of large houses to shut out the light for which they were too poor to pay.

* * * * *

Let us enter by the front door. We step into a spacious hall, innocent of carpet. There is a great fireplace, and over it a painting of David, and the Philistines, and Giant Goliath. The hall-floor was of brick, and carefully sprinkled with fresh sand. We see this in the country still, but not often in the minister's house. In the hall stood "the child's" rocking-horse. It was a grey horse, and could be ridden astride or side-saddle. When I visited Stambourne, in the year 1889, a man claimed to have rocked me upon it. I remembered the horse, but not the man,—so sadly do we forget the better, and remember the baser. This was the only horse that I ever enjoyed riding. Living animals are too eccentric in their movements, and the law of gravitation usually draws me from my seat upon them to a lower level; therefore I am not an inveterate lover of horseback. I can, however, testify of my Stambourne steed, that it was a horse on which even a member of Parliament might have retained his seat.

How I used to delight to stand in the hall, with the door open, and watch the rain run off the top of the door into a wash-tub! How much better to catch the overflow of the rain in a tub than to have a gutter to carry it off! So I thought; but do not now think. What bliss to float cotton-reels in the miniature sea! How fresh and sweet that rain seemed to be! The fragrance of the water which poured down in a thunder-shower comes over me now.

Where the window is open on the right, was the best parlour. Roses generally grew about it, and bloomed *in the room* if they could find means to insert their buds between the wall and the window-frame. They generally found ample space, for nothing was quite on the square. There had evidently been a cleaning up just before my photograph was taken, for there are no roses creeping up from below. What Vandals people are when they set about clearing up either the outsides or the insides of houses! On the sacred walls of this "best parlour" hung portraits of my grandparents and uncles, and on a piece of furniture stood the fine large basin which grandfather used for what he called "baptisms." In my heart of hearts, I believe it was originally intended for a punch-bowl; but, in any case, it was a work of art, worthy of the use to which it was dedicated. This is the room which contained the marvel to which I have often referred,—

AN APPLE IN A BOTTLE.

I remember well, in my early days, seeing upon my grandmother's mantel-shelf an apple contained in a phial. This was a great wonder to me, and I tried to investigate it. My question was, "How came the apple to get inside so small a bottle?" The apple was quite as big round as the phial; by what means was it placed within it? Though it was treason to touch the treasures on the mantel-piece, I took down the bottle, and convinced my youthful mind that the apple never passed through its neck; and by means of an attempt to unscrew the bottom, I became equally certain that the apple did not enter from below. I held to the notion that by some occult means the bottle had been made in two pieces, and afterwards united in so careful a manner that no trace of the join remained. I was hardly satisfied with the theory, but as no philosopher was at hand to suggest any other hypothesis, I let the matter rest. One day, the next summer, I chanced to see upon a bough another phial, the first cousin of my old friend, within which was growing a little apple which had been passed through the neck of the bottle while it was extremely small. "Nature well known, no prodigies remain." The grand secret was out. I did not cry, *"Eureka! Eureka!"* but I might have done so if I had then been versed in the Greek tongue.

This discovery of my juvenile days shall serve for an illustration at the present moment. Let us get the apples into the bottle while they are little: which, being translated, signifies, let us bring the young ones into the house of God, by means of the Sabbath-school, in the hope that, in after days, they will love the place where His honour dwelleth, and there seek and find eternal life. By our making the Sabbath dreary, many young minds may be prejudiced against religion: we would do the reverse. Sermons should not be so long and dull as to weary the young folk, or mischief will come of them; but with interesting preaching to secure attention, and loving teachers to press home the truth upon the youthful heart, we shall not have to complain of the next generation, that they have "forgotten their resting-places."

* * * * *

In this best parlour grandfather would usually sit on Sunday mornings, and prepare himself for preaching. I was put into the room with him that I might be quiet, and, as a rule, *The Evangelical Magazine* was given me. This contained a portrait of a reverend divine, and one picture of a mission-station. Grandfather often requested me to be quiet, and always gave as a reason that I "had the magazine." I did not at the time perceive the full force of the argument to be derived from that fact; but no doubt my venerable relative knew more about the sedative effect of the magazine than I did. I cannot support his opinion from personal experience. Another means of stilling "the child" was much more effectual. I was warned that perhaps grandpa would not be able to preach if I distracted him, and then,—ah! then, what would happen, if poor people did not learn the way to Heaven? This made me look at the portrait and the missionary-station once more. Little did I dream that some other child would one day see my face in that wonderful Evangelical portrait-gallery.

* * * * *

Yrs most affectionately,

Stambowm   C H Spurgeon

When I was a very small boy, I was allowed to read the
Scriptures at family prayer. Once upon a time, when reading the
passage in Revelation which mentions the bottomless pit, I paused,
and said, "Grandpa, what can this mean?" The answer was kind,
but unsatisfactory, "Pooh, pooh, child, go on." The child, however,
intended to have an explanation, and therefore selected the same
chapter morning after morning, and always halted at the same verse
to repeat the enquiry, hoping that by repetition he would importune
the good old gentleman into a reply. The process was successful,
for it is by no means the most edifying thing in the world to hear
the history of the Mother of Harlots, and the beast with seven
heads, every morning in the week, Sunday included, with no sort
of alternation either of Psalm or Gospel; the venerable patriarch
of the household therefore capitulated at discretion, with, "Well,
dear, what is it that puzzles you?" Now "the child" had often
seen baskets with but very frail bottoms, which in course of wear
became bottomless, and allowed the fruit placed therein to drop
upon the ground; here, then, was the puzzle,—if the pit aforesaid

had no bottom, where would all those people fall to who dropped out at its lower end?—a puzzle which rather startled the propriety of family worship, and had to be laid aside for explanation at some more convenient season. Queries of the like simple but rather unusual stamp would frequently break up into paragraphs of a miscellaneous length the Bible-reading of the assembled family, and had there not been a world of love and license allowed to the inquisitive reader, he would very soon have been deposed from his office. As it was, the Scriptures were not very badly rendered, and were probably quite as interesting as if they had not been interspersed with original and curious enquiries.

I can remember the horror of my mind when my dear grandfather told me what his idea of "the bottomless pit" was. There is a deep pit, and the soul is falling down,—oh, how fast it is falling! There! the last ray of light at the top has disappeared, and it falls on— on—on, and so it goes on falling—on—on—on for a thousand years! "Is it not getting near the bottom yet? Won't it stop?" No, no, the cry is, "On—on—on." "I have been falling a million years ; am I not near the bottom yet?" No, you are no nearer the bottom yet; it is "the *bottomless* pit." It is on—on—on, and so the soul goes on falling perpetually into a deeper depth still, falling for ever into "the bottomless pit"—on— on—on—into the pit that has no bottom! Woe, without termination, without hope of its coming to a conclusion!

∗ ∗ ∗ ∗ ∗

THE YEW HEDGE, STAMBOURNE.

In my grandfather's garden there was a fine old hedge of yew, of considerable length, which was clipped and trimmed till it made quite a wall of verdure. Behind it was a wide grass walk, which looked upon the fields; the grass was kept mown, so as to make pleasant walking. Here, ever since the old Puritanic chapel was built, godly divines had walked, and prayed, and meditated. My grandfather was wont to use it as his study. Up and down it he would walk when preparing his sermons, and always on Sabbath-days when it was fair, he had half-an-hour there before preaching. To me, it seemed to be a perfect paradise; and being forbidden to stay there when grandfather was meditating, I viewed it with no small degree of awe. I love to think of the green and quiet walk at this moment; but I was once shocked and even horrified by hearing a farming man remark concerning this *sanctum sanctorum,* "It 'ud grow a many 'taturs if it wor ploughed up." What cared he for holy memories? What were meditation and contemplation to him? Is it not the chief end of man to grow potatoes, and eat them? Such, on a larger scale, would be an unconverted man's estimate of joys so, elevated and refined as those of Heaven. Alphonse Karr tells a story of a servant-man who asked his master to be allowed to leave his cottage, and sleep over the stable. What was the matter with his cottage? "Why, Sir, the nightingales all around the cottage make such a 'jug, jug, jug,' at night that I cannot bear them." A man with a musical ear would be charmed with the nightingales' song, but here was a man without a musical soul who found the sweetest notes a nuisance. This is a feeble image of the incapacity of unregenerate man for the enjoyments of the world to come, and as he is incapable of enjoying them, so is he incapable of longing for them.

* * * * *

While my grandfather was preacher at the meeting-house, Mr. Hopkins was Rector at the church. They preached the same gospel, and without surrendering their principles, were great friends. The Bible Society held its meetings alternately in connection with the church and the meetinghouse. At times, the leading resident went to church in the morning, and to chapel in the afternoon; and, when I was a boy, I have, on Monday, gone to the Squire's to tea, with Mr. Hopkins and my grandfather. The glory of that tea-party was that we four, the three old gentlemen, and the little boy, *all ate sugared bread and butter together for a treat.* The sugar was very brown, but the young boy was very pleased, and the old boys were merry also. Yes, Stambourne had its choice pleasures!

It is pleasant to read of the harmony between these two men of God: they increased in mutual esteem as they increased in years. As Mr. Hopkins had more of the meat, and Mr. Spurgeon more of the mouths, the Rector did not forget to help his friend in divers quiet ways; such as a five-pound note for a sick daughter to go to the sea-side, and presents of comforts in illness. On one occasion, it is said that, having a joint of beef on the Rectory table, the clergyman cut it in halves, and sent his man on horseback with one half of it to the Independent Parsonage, while it was yet hot,—a kind of joke not often practised between established and dissenting ministers.

* * * * *

In the front of the house, towards the left, nearly hidden by a shrub, is a very important window, for it let light into the room wherein were the oven, the mangle, and, best of all, the kneading-trough. How often have I gone to that kneading-trough; for it had a little shelf in it, and there would be placed *"something for the child!"* A bit of pastry, which was called by me, according to its size, a pig or a rabbit, which had little ears, and two currants for eyes, was carefully placed in that sacred shrine, like the manna in the ark. Dear grandmother, how much you laboured to spoil that "child"! Yet your memory is more dear to him than that of wiser folks, who did not spoil "the child." Do you now look down from your mansion above upon your petted Grandson? Do you feel as if he would have been better if you had been sour and hard? Not a bit of it. Aunt Ann, who had a finger in it all, would spoil "the child" again if she had a chance. I have put in such an approach to a portrait of my grandmother as I could find: it was taken by some travelling artist who visited the district, and took off several of the family.

MY GRANDMOTHER.

The dairy at the back of the house was by no means a bad place for a cheesecake, or for a drink of cool milk. It makes one think of the hymn,—

"I have been there; and still would go."

The cupboard under the stairs, where they kept the sand for the floors, would be a real Old Curiosity Shop nowadays; but there it was, and great was the use of it to the cottagers around.

There was a sitting-room at the back of the house, where the family met for meals. In that which looks like a blank side in our picture there certainly was a window looking out upon the garden; perhaps it was a little further back than the picture goes. A very pleasant outlook there was from that window down the green garden paths, and over the hedge into the road. When I last saw the "keeping-room," a bit of ivy had forced its way through the lath and plaster, and had been trained along the inside of the room; but in my childish days we were not so verdant. I remember a mark on the paper which had been made by the finger of one of my uncles, so they told me, when one year the flour was so bad that it turned into a paste, or pudding, inside the loaf, and could not be properly made into bread. History has before this been learned from handwritings on the wall. The times of the old Napoleon wars, and of the Corn Laws, must often have brought straitness of bread into the household; and a failure in the yield of the little farm made itself felt in the family.

There was a mysterious jack over the fire-place, and with that fire-place itself I was very familiar; for candles were never used extravagantly in grandfather's house, and if anyone went out of the room, and took the candle with him, it was just a little darker, not very much; and if one wished to read, the fire-light was the only resort. There were mould candies now and then in the best room, but that was only on very high days and holidays. My opinion, derived from personal observation, was that all every-day-candles were made of rushes and tallow.

Our young readers in London and other large towns have probably never seen a pair of snuffers, much less the flint and steel with which a light had to be painfully obtained by the help of a tinder-box and a brimstone match. What a job on a cold raw morning to strike, and strike, and see the sparks die out because the tinder was damp! We are indeed living in an age of light when we compare our incandescent gas-burners and electric lights with the rushlights of our childhood. And yet the change is not all one way; for if we have more light, we have also more fog and smoke, at least in London. Our "keeping-room" was a very nice, large, comfortable dining-room, and it had a large store-closet at one end. You should have seen the best china! It only came out on state occasions, but it was very marvellous in "the child's" eyes.

A quaint old winding stair led to the upper chambers. The last time I occupied the best bedroom, the floor appeared anxious to go out of the window, at least, it inclined that way. There seemed to be a chirping of birds very near my pillow in the morning, and I discovered that swallows had built outside the plaster, and sparrows had found a hole which admitted them inside of it, that there they might lay their young. It is not always that one can lie in bed and study ornithology. I confess that I liked all this rural life, and the old chintz bed-furniture, and the paper round the looking-glass cut in the form of horse-chestnut leaves and dahlias, and the tottery old mansion altogether.

* * * * *

THE BOY AMONG THE BOOKS.

I am afraid I am amusing myself rather than my reader, and so I will not weary him with more than this one bit more of rigmarole just now. But there was one place upstairs which I cannot omit, even at the risk of being wearisome. Opening out of one of the bedrooms, there was a little chamber of which the window had been blocked up through that wretched window-duty. When the original founder of Stambourne Meeting quitted the Church of England, to form a separate congregation, he would seem to have been in possession of a fair estate, and the house was quite a noble one for those times. Before the light-excluding tax had come into operation, that little room was the minister's study and closet for prayer; and a very nice cosy room, too. In my time, it was a dark den;—but *it contained books,* and this made it a gold mine to me. Therein was fulfilled the promise, "I will give thee the treasures of darkness." Some of these were enormous folios, such as a boy could hardly lift. Here I first struck up acquaintance with the martyrs, and specially with "Old Bonner," who burned them; next, with Bunyan and his "Pilgrim"; and further on, with the great masters of Scriptural theology, with whom no moderns are worthy to be named in the same day. Even the old editions of their works, with their margins and old-fashioned notes, are precious to me. It is easy to tell a real Puritan book even by its shape and by the appearance of the type. I confess that I harbour a prejudice against nearly all new editions, and cultivate a preference for the originals, even though they wander about in sheepskins and goatskins, or are shut up in the hardest of boards. It made my eyes water, a short time ago, to see a number of these old books in the new Manse: I wonder whether some other boy will love them, and live to revive that grand old divinity which will yet be to England her balm and benison.

Out of that darkened room I fetched those old authors when I was yet a youth, and never was I happier than when in their company. Out of the present contempt, into which Puritanism has fallen, many brave hearts and true will fetch it, by the help of God, ere many years have passed. Those who have daubed up the windows will yet be surprised to see Heaven's light beaming on the old truth, and then breaking forth from it to their own confusion.

* * * * *

(The following incident in Mr. Spurgeon's childhood's days is here given as it was related by his "Aunt Ann" on the occasion when he visited Stambourne in the summer of 1887.

One of the members of the church at Stambourne, named Roads, was in the habit of frequenting the public-house to have his "drop of beer", and smoke his pipe, greatly to the grief of his godly pastor, who often heaved a sigh at the thought of his unhappy member's inconsistent conduct. Little Charles had doubtless noticed his grandfather's grief on this account, and laid it to heart. One day he suddenly exclaimed, in the hearing of the good old gentleman, "I'll kill old Roads, that I will!" "Hush, hush! my dear," said the good pastor, "you mustn't talk so; it's very wrong, you know, and you'll get taken up by the police, if you do anything wrong." "I shall not do anything bad; but I'll kill him though, that I will." Well, the good grandfather was puzzled, but yet perfectly sure that the child would not do anything which he knew to be wrong, so he let it pass with some half-mental remark about "that strange child." Shortly after, however, the above conversation was brought to his mind by the child coming in and saying, "I've killed old Roads; he'll never grieve my dear grandpa any more." "My dear child," said the good man, "what have you done? Where have you been?" "I haven't been doing any harm, grandpa," said the child; "I've been about the Lord's work, that's all."

Nothing more could be elicited from little Charles; but, before long, the mystery was cleared up. "Old Roads" called to see his pastor, and, with downcast looks and evident sorrow of heart, narrated the story of how he had been killed, somewhat in this fashion:—"I'm very sorry indeed, my dear pastor, to have caused you such grief and trouble. It was very wrong, I know; but I always loved you, and wouldn't have done it if I'd only thought." Encouraged by the good pastor's kindly Christian words, he went on with his story. "I was a-sitting in the public just having my pipe and mug of beer, when that child comes in,—to think an old man like me should be took to task, and reproved by a bit of a child like that! Well, he points at me with his finger, just so, and says, 'What doest thou here, Elijah? sitting with the ungodly; and you a member of a church, and breaking your pastor's heart. I'm ashamed of you! I wouldn't break my pastor's heart, I'm sure.' And then he walks away. Well, I did feel angry; but I knew it was all true, and I was guilty; so I put down my pipe, and did not touch my beer, but hurried away to a lonely spot, and cast myself down before the Lord, confessing my sin and begging for forgiveness. And I do know and believe the Lord in mercy pardoned me; and now I've come to ask you to forgive me; and I'll never grieve you any more, my dear pastor." It need not be said that the penitent was freely forgiven, and owned a brother in the Lord, and the Lord was praised for the wonderful way in which it had all come about.)

(The genuineness of the backslider's restoration is evident from the testimony of Mr. Houchin, the minister at Stambourne who succeeded Mr. Spurgeon's grandfather, and who has also ascertained from official records the correct way of spelling "Old Roads"' name. Mr. Houchin writes:—

"Thomas Roads was one of the old men of the table-pew,— an active, lively, little man, but quite illiterate,—not much above a labourer, but he kept a pony and cart, and did a little buying and selling on his own account . . . I found him an earnest and zealous Christian, striving to be useful in every way possible to him; especially in the prayer-meetings and among the young people, opening his house for Christian conversation and prayer. He only lived about four years of my time, and was sustained with a cheerful confidence to the end. When near death, on my taking up the Bible to read and pray with him, he said, 'I have counted the leaves, sir.' I said, 'Why! what did you do that for?' and he replied, 'I never could read a word of it, and thought I would know how many leaves there were.' This was very pathetic, and revealed much. We had a good hope of him, and missed him greatly.")

THE KIND OF REVIVAL WE NEED

IT IS GOOD for us to draw nigh unto God in prayer. Our minds are grieved to see so little attention given to united prayer by many churches.

How can we expect a blessing if we are too idle to ask for it? How can we look for a Pentecost if we never meet with one another, in one place, to wait upon the Lord? Brethren, we shall never see much change for the better in our churches till the prayer meeting occupies a higher place in the esteem of Christians.

But now that we have come together, how shall we pray? Let us not degenerate into formality, or we shall be dead while we think we live. Let us not waiver through unbelief, or we shall pray in vain. Oh, for great faith with which to offer great prayers!

We have been mingling praise and prayer together as a delicious compound of spices, fit to be presented upon the altar of incense through Christ our Lord; may we not at this time offer some special far-reaching petition? It is suggested to me that we pray for a true and genuine revival of religion throughout the world.

A Real and Lasting Revival

I am glad of any signs of life, even if they should be feverish and transient, and I am slow to judge any well intended movement, but I am very fearful that many so called revivals in the long run wrought more harm than good. A species of religious gambling has fascinated many men, and given them a distaste for the sober business of true godliness.

But if I would nail down counterfeits upon the counter, I do not therefore undervalue true gold. Far from it. It is to be desired beyond measure that the Lord would send a real and lasting revival of spiritual life.

We need a work of the Holy Spirit of a supernatural kind, putting power into the preaching of the Word, inspiring all believers with heavenly energy, and solemnly affecting the hearts of the careless, so that they turn to God and live. We would not be drunk with the wine of carnal excitement, but we would be filled with the Spirit. We would behold the fire descending from heaven in answer to the effectual fervent prayers of righteous men. Can we not entreat the Lord our God to make bare His holy arm in the eyes of all the people in this day of declension and vanity?

Old-fashioned Doctrine

We want a revival of old-fashioned doctrine. I know not a single doctrine which is not at this hour studiously undermined by those who ought to be its defenders. There is not a truth that is precious to the soul which is not now denied by those whose profession it is to proclaim it. To me it is clear that we need a revival of old-fashioned gospel preaching like that of Whitefield and Wesley.

The Scriptures must be made the infallible foundation of all teaching; the ruin, redemption and regeneration of mankind must be set forth in unmistakable terms.

Personal Godliness

Urgently do we need a revival of personal godliness. This is, indeed, the secret of church prosperity. When individuals fall from their steadfastness, the church is tossed to and fro; when personal faith is steadfast, the church abides true to her Lord.

It is upon the truly godly and spiritual that the future of religion depends in the hand of God. Oh, for more truly holy men, quickened and filled with the Holy Spirit, consecrated to the Lord and sanctified by His truth.

Brethren, we must each one live if the church is to be alive; we must live unto God if we expect to see the pleasure of the Lord prospering in our hands. Sanctified men are the salt of society and the saviours of the race.

Domestic Religion

We deeply want a revival of domestic religion. The Christian family was the bulwark of godliness in the days of the puritans, but in these evil times hundreds of families of so-called Christians have no family worship, no restraint upon growing sons, and no wholesome instruction or discipline. How can we hope to see the kingdom of our Lord advance when His own disciples do not teach His gospel to their own children?

Oh, Christian men and women, be thorough in what you do and know and teach! Let your families be trained in the fear of God and be yourselves "holiness unto the Lord"; so shall you stand like a rock amid the surging waves of error and ungodliness which rage around us.

Vigorous, Consecrated Strength

We want also a revival of vigorous, consecrated strength. I have pleaded for true piety; I now beg for one of the highest results of it. We need saints. We need gracious minds trained to a high form of spiritual life by much converse with God in solitude.

Saints acquire nobility from their constant resort to the place where the Lord meets with them. There they also acquire that power in prayer which we so greatly need. Oh, that we had more men like John Knox, whose prayers were more terrible to Queen Mary than 10,000 men! Oh, that we had more Elijahs by whose faith the windows of heavens should be shut or opened!

This power comes not by a sudden effort; it is the outcome of a life devoted to the God of Israel! If our life is all in public, it will be a frothy, vapoury ineffectual existence; but if we hold high converse with God in secret, we shall be mighty for good. He that is a prince with God will take high rank with men, after the true measure of nobility.

Beware of being a lean-to; endeavour to rest on your own walls of real faith in the Lord Jesus. May none of us fall into a mean, poverty-stricken dependence on man! We want among us believers like those solid, substantial family mansions which stand from generation to generation as landmarks of the country; no lath-and-plaster fabrics, but edifices solidly constructed to bear all weathers, and defy time itself.

Given a host of men who are steadfast, immovable, always abounding in the work of the Lord, the glory of God's grace will be clearly manifested, not only in them, but in those round about them. The Lord send us a revival of consecrated strength, and heavenly energy!

Preach by your hands if you cannot preach by your tongues. When our church members show the fruits of true godliness, we shall soon have inquiries for the tree which bears such a crop.

Oh the coming together of the saints is the first part of Pentecost, and the ingathering of sinners is the second. It began with "only a prayer meeting", but it ended with a grand baptism of thousands of converts. Oh that the prayers of believers may act as lode stones to sinners! Oh that every gathering of faithful men might be a lure to attract others to Jesus! May many souls fly to Him because they see others speeding in that direction.

"Lord, we turn from these poor foolish procrastinators to thyself, and we plead for them with thine all-wise and gracious spirit! Lord, turn them and they shall be turned! By their conversion, pray that a true revival has commenced tonight! Let it spread through all our households, and then run from church to church till the whole of christendom shall be ablaze with a heaven-descended fire!"

THE GREAT CHANGE—CONVERSION

I have heard men tell the story of their conversion, and of their spiritual life, in such a way that my heart hath loathed them and their story, too, for they have told of their sins as if they did boast in the greatness of their crime, and they have mentioned the love of God, not with a tear of gratitude, not with the simple thanksgiving of the really humble heart, but as if they as much exalted themselves as they exalted God. Oh! when we tell the story of our own conversion, I would have it done with great sorrow, remembering what we used to be, and with great joy and gratitude, remembering how little we deserve these things. I was once preaching upon conversion and salvation, and I felt within myself, as preachers often do, that it was but dry work to tell this story, and a dull, dull tale it was to me; but, on a sudden, the thought crossed my mind, "Why, you are a poor, lost, ruined sinner yourself; tell it, tell it as you received it; begin to tell of the grace of God as you trust you feel it yourself." Why, then, my eyes began to be fountains of tears; those hearers who had nodded their heads began to brighten up, and they listened, because they were hearing something which the speaker himself felt, and which they recognized as being true to him if it was not true to them.

Can you not remember, dearly-beloved, that day of days, that best and brightest of hours, when first you saw the Lord, lost your burden, received the roll of promise, rejoiced in full salvation, and went on your way in peace? My soul can never forget that day. Dying, all but dead, diseased, pained, chained, scourged, bound in fetters of iron, in darkness and the shadow of death, Jesus appeared unto me. My eyes looked to Him; the disease was healed, the pains removed, chains were snapped, prison doors were opened, darkness gave place to light. What delight filled my soul!—what mirth, what ecstasy, what sound of music and dancing, what soarings towards Heaven, what heights and depths of ineffable delight! Scarcely ever since then have I known joys which surpassed the rapture of that first hour.—C. H. S.

* * * * *

LET our lips crowd sonnets within the compass of a word; let our voice distil hours of melody into a single syllable; let our tongue utter in one letter the essence of the harmony of ages; for we write of an hour which as far excelleth all other days of our life as gold exceedeth dross. As the night of Israel's passover was a night to be remembered, a theme for bards, and an incessant fountain of grateful song, even so is the time of which we now tell, the never-to-be-forgotten hour of our emancipation from guilt, and our justification in Jesus. Other days have mingled with their fellows till, like coins worn in circulation, their image and superscription are entirely obliterated; but this day remaineth new, fresh, bright, as distinct in all its parts as if it were but yesterday struck from the mint of time. Memory shall drop from the palsied hand full many a memento which now she cherishes, but she shall never, even when she tottereth to the grave, unbind from her heart the token of the thrice-happy hour of the redemption of our spirit. The emancipated galley-slave may forget the day which heard his broken fetters rattle on the ground; the pardoned traitor may fail to remember the moment when the axe of the headsman was averted by a pardon; and the long-despairing mariner may not recollect the moment when a friendly hand snatched him from the hungry deep; but O hour of forgiven sin, moment of perfect pardon, our soul shall never forget thee while within her life and being find an immortality! Each day of our life hath had its attendant angel; but on this day, like Jacob at Mahanaim, hosts of angels met us. The sun hath risen every morning, but on that eventful morn he had the light or seven days. As the days of Heaven upon earth, as the years of immortality, as the ages of glory, as the bliss of Heaven, so were the hours of that thrice-happy day. Rapture divine, and ecstasy inexpressible, filled our soul. Fear, distress, and grief, with all their train of woes, fled hastily away; and in their place joys came without number.

When I was in the hand of the Holy Spirit, under conviction of sin, I had a clear and sharp sense of the justice of God. Sin, whatever it might be to other people, became to me an intolerable burden. It was not so much that I feared hell, as that I feared sin; and all the while, I had upon my mind a deep concern for the honour of God's name, and the integrity of His moral government. I felt that it would not satisfy my conscience if I could be forgiven unjustly. But then there came the question,—"How could God be just, and yet justify me who had been so guilty?" I was worried and wearied with this question; neither could I see any answer to it. Certainly, I could never have invented an answer which would have satisfied my conscience. The doctrine of the atonement is to my mind one of the surest proofs of the Divine inspiration of Holy Scripture. Who would or could have thought of the just Ruler dying for the unjust rebel? This is no teaching of human mythology, or dream of poetical imagination. This method of expiation is only known among men because it is a fact: fiction could not have devised it. God Himself ordained it; it is not a matter which could have been imagined.

I had heard of the plan of salvation by the sacrifice of Jesus from my youth up but I did not know any more about it in my innermost soul than if I had been born and bred a Hottentot. The light was there, but I was blind: it was of necessity that the Lord Himself should make the matter plain to me. It came to me as a new revelation, as fresh as if I had never read in Scripture that Jesus was declared to be the propitiation for sins that God might be just. I believe it will have to come as a revelation to every new-born child of God whenever he sees it; I mean that glorious doctrine of the substitution of the Lord Jesus. I came to understand that salvation was possible through vicarious sacrifice; and that provision had been made in the first constitution and arrangement of things for such a substitution. I was made to see that He who is the Son of God, co-equal, and co-eternal with the Father, had of old been made the covenant Head of a chosen people, that He might in that capacity suffer for them and save them. Inasmuch as our fall was not at the first a personal one, for we fell in our federal representative, the first Adam, it became possible for us to be recovered by a second Representative, even by Him who has undertaken to be the covenant Head of His people, so as to be their second Adam. I saw that, ere I actually sinned, I had fallen by my first father's sin; and I rejoiced that, therefore, it became possible in point of law for me to rise by a second Head and Representative. The fall by Adam left a loophole of escape; another Adam could undo the ruin wrought by the first.

When I was anxious about the possibility of a just God pardoning me, I understood and saw by faith that He who is the Son of God became man, and in His own blessed person bore my sin in His own body on the tree. I saw that the chastisement of my peace was laid on Him, and that with His stripes I was healed. It was because the Son of God, supremely glorious in His matchless person, undertook to vindicate the law by bearing the sentence due to me, that therefore God was able to pass by my sin. My sole hope for Heaven lies in the full atonement made upon Calvary's cross for the ungodly. On that I firmly rely. I have not the shadow of a hope anywhere else. Personally, I could never have overcome my own sinfulness. I tried and failed. My evil propensities were too many for me, till, in the belief that Christ died for me, I cast my guilty soul on Him, and then I received a conquering principle by which I overcame my sinful self. The doctrine of the cross can be used to slay sin, even as the old warriors used their huge two-handed swords, and mowed down their foes at every stroke. There is nothing like faith in the sinners' Friend: it overcomes all evil. If Christ has died for me, ungodly as I am, without strength as I am, then I cannot live in sin any longer, but must arouse myself to love and serve Him who hath redeemed me. I cannot trifle with the evil which slew my best Friend. I must be holy for His sake. How can I live in sin when He has died to save me from it?

There was a day, as I took my walks abroad, when I came hard by a spot for ever engraven upon my memory, for there I saw this Friend, my best, my only Friend, murdered. I stooped down in sad affright, and looked at Him. I saw that His hands had been pierced with rough iron nails, and His feet had been rent in the same way. There was misery in His dead countenance so terrible that I scarcely dared to look upon it. His body was emaciated with hunger, His back was red with bloody scourges, and His brow had a circle of wounds about it: clearly could one see that these had been pierced by thorns. I shuddered, for I had known this Friend full well. He never had a fault; He was the purest of the pure, the holiest of the holy. Who could have injured Him? For He never injured any man: all His life long He "went about doing good;" He had healed the sick, He had fed the hungry, He had raised the dead: for which of these works did they kill Him? He had never breathed out anything else but love; and as I looked into the poor sorrowful face, so full of agony, and yet so full of love, I wondered who could have been a wretch so vile as to pierce hands like His. I said within myself, "Where can these traitors live? Who are these that could have smitten such an One as this? Had they murdered an oppressor, we might have forgiven them; had they slain one who had indulged in vice or villainy, it might have been his desert; had it been a murderer and a rebel, or one who had committed sedition, we would have said, "Bury his corpse: justice has at last given him his due." But when Thou wast slain, my best, my only-beloved, where lodged the traitors? Let me seize them, and they shall be put to death. If there be torments that I can devise, surely they shall endure them all. Oh! what jealousy; what revenge I felt! If I might but find these murderers, what would I not do with them! And as I looked upon that corpse, I heard a footstep, and wondered where it was. I listened, and I clearly perceived that the murderer was close at hand. It was dark, and I groped about to find him. I found that, somehow or other, wherever I put out my hand, I could not meet with him, for he was nearer to me than my hand would go. At last I put my hand upon my breast. "I have thee now," said I; for lo! he was in my own heart; the murderer was hiding within my own bosom, dwelling in the recesses of my inmost soul. Ah! then I wept indeed, that I, in the very presence of my murdered Master, should be harbouring the murderer; and I felt myself most guilty while I bowed over His corpse, and sang that plaintive hymn,—

> "'Twas you, my sins, my cruel sins,
>   His chief tormentors were;
> Each of my crimes became a nail,
>   And unbelief the spear."

Amid the rabble rout which hounded the Redeemer to His doom, there were some gracious souls whose bitter anguish sought vent in wailing and lamentations,—fit music to accompany that march of woe. When my soul can, in imagination, see the Saviour bearing His cross to Calvary, she joins the godly women, and weeps with them; for, indeed, there is true cause for grief,—cause lying deeper than those mourning women thought. They bewailed innocence maltreated, goodness persecuted, love bleeding, meekness about to die; but my heart has a deeper and more bitter cause to mourn. My sins were the scourges which lacerated those blessed shoulders, and crowned with thorns those bleeding brows: my sins cried, "Crucify Him! Crucify Him!" and laid the cross upon His gracious shoulders. His being led forth to die is sorrow enough for one eternity; but my having been His murderer, is more, infinitely more grief than one poor fountain of tears can express.

Why those women loved and wept, it were not hard to guess; but they could not have had greater reasons for love and grief than my heart has. Nain's widow saw her son restored; but I myself have been raised to newness of life. Peter's wife's mother was cured of the fever; but I of the greater plague of sin. Out of Magdalene seven devils were cast;—but a whole legion out of me. Mary and Martha were favoured with visits from Him; but He dwells with me. His mother bare His body; but He is formed in me, "the hope of glory." In nothing behind the holy women in debt, let me not be behind them in gratitude or sorrow.

> Love and grief my heart dividing,
>   With my tears His feet I'll lave
>   Constant still in heart abiding,
>   Weep for Him who died to save."

William Huntingdon says, in his autobiography, that one of the sharpest sensations of pain that he felt, after he had been quickened by Divine grace, was this, "He felt such pity for God." I do not know that I ever met with the expression elsewhere, but it is a very striking one; although I might prefer to say that I have sympathy with God, and grief that He should be treated so ill. Ah, there are many men that are forgotten, that are despised, and that are trampled on by their fellows; but there never was a man who was so despised as the everlasting God has been! Many a man has been slandered and abused, but never was man abused as God has been. Many have been treated cruelly and ungratefully, but never was one treated as our God has been. I, too, once despised Him. He knocked at the door of my heart, and I refused to open it, He came to me, times without number, morning by morning, and night by night; He checked me in my conscience, and spoke to me by His Spirit, and when, at last, the thunders of the law prevailed in my conscience, I thought that Christ was cruel and unkind. Oh, I can never forgive myself that I should have thought so ill of Him! But what a loving reception did I have when I went to Him! I thought He would smite me, but His hand was not clenched in anger, but opened wide in mercy. I thought full sure that His eyes would dart lightning-flashes of wrath upon me; but, instead thereof, they were full of tears. He fell upon my neck, and kissed me; He took off my rags, and did clothe me with His righteousness, and caused my soul to sing aloud for joy; while in the house of my heart, and in the house of His Church, there was music and dancing, because His son that He had lost was found, and he that had been dead was made alive again.

There is a power in God's gospel beyond all description. Once I, like Mazeppa, lashed to the wild horse of my lust, bound hand and foot, incapable of resistance, was galloping on with hell's wolves behind me, howling for my body and my soul as their just and lawful prey. There came a mighty hand which stopped that wild horse, cut my bands, set me down, and brought me into liberty. Is there power in the gospel? Ay, there is, and he who has felt it must acknowledge it. There was a time when I lived in the strong old castle of my sins, and rested in my own works. There came a trumpeter to the door, and bade me open it. I with anger chid him from the porch, and said he ne'er should enter. Then there came a goodly Personage, with loving countenance; His hands were marked with scars where nails had been driven, and His feet had nail-prints, too. He lifted up His cross, using it as a hammer; at the first blow, the gate of my prejudice shook; at the second, it trembled more; at the third, down it fell, and in He came; and He said, "Arise, and stand upon thy feet, for I have loved thee with an everlasting love." The gospel a thing of power! Ah! that it is. It always wears the dew of its youth; it glitters with morning's freshness, its strength and its glory abide for ever. I have felt its power in my own heart; I have the witness of the Spirit within my spirit, and I know it is a thing of might, because it has conquered me, and bowed me down.

> "His free grace alone, from the first to the last,
> Hath won my affections, and bound my soul fast."

In my conversion, the very point lay in making the discovery that I had nothing to do but to look to Christ, and I should be saved. I believe that I had been a very good, attentive hearer; my own impression about myself was that nobody ever listened much better than I did. For years, as a child, I tried to learn the way of salvation; and either I did not hear it set forth, which I think cannot quite have been the case, or else I was spiritually blind and deaf, and could not see it and could not hear it; but the good news that I was, as a sinner, to look away from myself to Christ, as much startled me, and came as fresh to me, as any news ever heard in my life. Had I never read my Bible? Yes, and read it earnestly. Had I never been taught by Christian people? Yes, I had, by mother, and father, and others. Had I not heard the gospel? Yes, I think I had; and yet, somehow, it was like a new revelation to me that I was to "believe and live." I confess to have been tutored in piety, put into my cradle by prayerful bands, and lulled to sleep by songs concerning Jesus; but after having heard the gospel continually, with line upon line, precept upon precept, here much and there much, yet, when the Word of the Lord came to me with power, it was as new as if I had lived amid the unvisited tribes of Central Africa, and had never heard the tidings of the cleansing fountain filled with blood, drawn from the Saviour's veins.

When, for the first time, I received the gospel to my soul's salvation, I thought that I had never really heard it before, and I began to think that the preachers to whom I had listened had not truly preached it. But, on looking back, I am inclined to believe that I had heard the gospel fully preached many hundreds of times before, and that this was the difference,—that I then heard it as though I heard it not; and when I did hear it, the message may not have been any more clear in itself than it had been at former times, but the power of the Holy Spirit was present to open my ear, and to guide the message to my heart. I have no doubt that I heard, scores of times, such texts as these,—"He that believeth and is baptized shall be saved;" "Look unto Me, and be ye saved, all the ends of the earth;" "As Moses lifted up the serpent in the wilderness, even so must the Son of man be lifted up: that whosoever believeth in Him should not perish, but have everlasting life;" yet I had no intelligent idea of what faith meant. When I first discovered what faith really was, and exercised it,—for with me these two things came together, I believed as soon as ever I knew what believing meant,—then I thought I had never before heard that truth preached. But, now, I am persuaded that the light often shone on my eyes, but I was blind, and therefore I thought that the light had never come there. The light was shining all the while, but there was no power to receive it; the eyeball of the soul was not sensitive to the Divine beams.

I could not believe that it was possible that *my* sins could be forgiven. I do not know why, but I seemed to be the odd person in the world. When the catalogue was made out, it appeared to me that, for some reason, I must have been left out. If God had saved me, and not the world, I should have wondered indeed; but if He had saved all the world except me, that would have seemed to me to be but right. And now, being saved by grace, I cannot help saying, "I am indeed a brand plucked out of the fire!" I believe that some of us who were kept by God a long while before we found Him, love Him better perhaps than we should have done if we had received Him directly; and we can preach better to others, we can speak more of His lovingkindness and tender mercy. John Bunyan could not have written as he did if he had not been dragged about by the devil for many years. I love that picture of dear old Christian. I know, when I first read *The Pilgrim's Progress,* and saw in it the woodcut of Christian carrying the burden on his back, I felt so interested in the poor fellow, that I thought I should jump with joy when, after he had carried his heavy load so long, he at last got rid of it; and that was how I felt when the burden of guilt, which I had borne so long, was for ever rolled away from my shoulders and my heart.

I can recollect when, like the poor dove sent out by Noah from his hand, I flew over the wide expanse of waters, and hoped to find some place where I might rest my wearied wing. Up towards the North I flew; and my eye looked keenly through the mist and darkness, if perhaps it might find some floating substance on which my soul might rest its foot, but it found nothing. Again it turned its wing, and flapped it, but not so rapidly as before, across that deep water that knew no shore; but still there was no rest. The raven had found its resting-place upon a floating body, and was feeding itself upon the carrion of some drowned man's carcass; but my poor soul found no rest. I flew on; I fancied I saw a ship sailing out at sea; it was the ship of the law; and I thought I would put my feet on its canvas, or rest myself on its cordage for a time, and find some refuge. But, ah! it was an airy phantom, on which I could not rest; for my foot had no right to rest on the law; I had not kept it, and the soul that keepeth it not, must die. At last I saw the barque *Christ Jesus,* that happy ark; and I thought I would fly thither; but my poor wing was weary, I could fly no further, and down I sank; but, as providence would have it, when my wings were flagging, and I was falling into the flood to be drowned, just below me was the roof of the ark, and I saw a hand put out from it, and One took hold of me, and said, "I have loved thee with an everlasting love, therefore I have not delivered the soul of My turtle-dove unto the multitude of the wicked; come in, come in!" Then I found that I had in my mouth an olive leaf of peace with God, and peace with man, plucked off by Jesus' mighty power.

Once, God preached to me by a similitude in the depth of winter. The earth had been black, and there was scarcely a green thing or a flower to be seen. As I looked across the fields, there was nothing but barrenness,—bare hedges and leafless trees, and black, black earth, wherever I gazed. On a sudden, God spake, and unlocked the treasures of the snow, and white flakes descended until there was no blackness to be seen, and all was one sheet of dazzling whiteness. It was at the time that I was seeking the Saviour, and not long before I found Him; and I remember well that sermon which I saw before me in the snow: "Come now, and let us reason together, saith the Lord: though your sins be as scarlet, they shall be as white as snow; though they be red like crimson, they shall be as wool."

Personally, I have to bless God for many good books; I thank Him for Dr. Doddridge's *Rise and Progress of Religion in the Soul;* for Baxter's *Call to the Unconverted;* for Alleine's *Alarm to Sinners;* and for James's *Anxious Enquirer;* but my gratitude most of all is due to God, not for books, but for the preached Word,—and that too addressed to me by a poor, uneducated man, a man who had never received any training for the ministry, and probably will never be heard of in this life, a man engaged in business, no doubt of a humble kind, during the week, but who had just enough of grace to say on the Sabbath, "Look unto Me, and be ye saved, all the ends of the earth." The books were good, but the man was better. The revealed Word awakened me; but it was the preached Word that saved me; and I must ever attach peculiar value to the *hearing of the truth,* for by it I received the joy and peace in which my soul delights. While under concern of soul, I resolved that I would attend all the places of worship in the town where I lived, in order that I might find out the way of salvation. I was willing to do anything, and be anything, if God would only forgive my sin. I set off, determined to go round to all the chapels, and I did go to every place of worship; but for a long time I went in vain. I do not, however, blame the ministers. One man preached Divine Sovereignty; I could hear him with pleasure, but what was that sublime truth to a poor sinner who wished to know what he must do to be saved? There was another admirable man who always preached about the law; but what was the use of ploughing up ground that needed to be sown? Another was a practical preacher. I heard him, but it was very much like a commanding officer teaching the manoeuvres of war to a set of men without feet. What could I do? All his exhortations were lost on me. I knew it, was said, "Believe on the Lord Jesus Christ, and thou shalt be saved;" but I did not know what it was to believe on Christ. These good men all preached truths suited to many in their congregations who were spiritually-minded people; but what I wanted to know was,—"How can I get my sins forgiven?"—and they never told me that. I desired to hear how a poor sinner, under a sense of sin, might find peace with God; and when I went, I heard a sermon on "Be not deceived, God is not mocked," which cut me up still worse; but did not bring me into rest. I went again, another day, and the text was something about the glories of the righteous; nothing for poor me! I was like a dog under the table, not allowed to eat of the children's food. I went time after time, and I can honestly say that I do not know that I ever went without prayer to God, and I am sure there was not a more attentive hearer than myself in all the place, for I panted and longed to understand how I might be saved.

I sometimes think I might have been in darkness and despair until now had it not been for the goodness of God in sending a snowstorm, one Sunday morning, while I was going to a certain place of worship. When I could go no further, I turned down a side street, and came to a little Primitive Methodist Chapel. In that chapel there may have been a dozen or fifteen people. I had heard of the Primitive Methodists, how they sang so loudly that they made people's heads ache; but that did not matter to me. I wanted to know how I might be saved, and if they could tell me that, I did not care how much they made my head ache. The minister did not come that morning; he was snowed up, I suppose. At last, a very thin-looking man,[1] a shoemaker, or tailor, or something of that sort, went up into the pulpit to preach. Now, it is well that preachers should be instructed; but this man was really stupid. He was obliged to stick to his text, for the simple reason that he had little else to say. The text was,—

"LOOK UNTO ME, AND BE YE SAVED, ALL THE ENDS OF THE EARTH."

He did not even pronounce the words rightly, but that did not matter. There was, I thought, a glimpse of hope for me in that text. The preacher began thus—"My dear friends, this is a very simple text indeed. It says, 'Look.' Now lookin' don't take a deal of pains. It ain't liftin' your foot or your finger; it is just, 'Look.' Well, a man needn't go to College to learn to look. You may be the biggest fool, and yet you can look. A man needn't be worth a thousand a year to be able to look. Anyone can look; even a child can look. But then the text says, 'Look unto *Me.*' Ay!" said he, in broad Essex, "many on ye are lookin' to yourselves, but it's no use lookin' there. You'll never find any comfort in yourselves. Some look to God the Father. No, look to Him by-and-by. Jesus Christ says, 'Look unto *Me.*' Some on ye say, 'We must wait for the Spirit's workin'.' You have no business with that just now. Look to *Christ.* The text says, 'Look unto *Me.*'"

Then the good man followed up his text in this way:—"Look unto Me; I am sweatin' great drops of blood. Look unto Me; I am hangin' on the cross. Look unto Me; I am dead and buried. Look unto Me; I rise again. Look unto Me; I ascend to Heaven. Look unto Me; I am sittin' at the Father's right hand. O poor sinner, look unto Me! look unto Me!

When he had gone to about that length, and managed to spin out ten minutes or so, he was at the end of his tether. Then he looked at me under the gallery, and I daresay, with so few present, he knew me to be a stranger. Just fixing his eyes on me, as if he knew all my heart, he said, "Young man, you look very miserable." Well, I did; but I had not been accustomed to have remarks made from the pulpit on my personal appearance before. However, it was a good blow, struck right home. He continued, "and you always will be miserable—miserable in life, and miserable in death,—if you don't obey my text; but if you obey now, this moment, you will be saved." Then, lifting up his hands, he shouted, as only a Primitive Methodist could do, "Young man, look to Jesus Christ. Look! Look! Look! You have nothin' to do but to look and live." I saw at once the way of salvation. I know not what else he said,—I did not take much notice of it,—I was so possessed with that one thought. Like as when the brazen serpent was lifted up, the people only looked and were healed, so it was with me. I had been waiting to do fifty things, but when I heard that word, "Look!" what a charming word it seemed to me! Oh! I looked until I could almost have looked my eyes away. There and then the cloud was gone, the darkness had rolled away, and that moment I saw the sun; and I could have risen that instant, and sung with the most enthusiastic of them, of the precious blood of Christ, and the simple faith which looks alone to Him. Oh, that somebody had told me this before, "Trust Christ, and you shall be saved." Yet it was, no doubt, all wisely ordered, and now I can say,—

> "Ever since by faith I saw the stream
> Thy flowing wounds supply,
> Redeeming love has been my theme,
> And shall be till I die."

I do from my soul confess that I never was satisfied till I came to Christ; when was yet a child, I had far more wretchedness than ever I have now; I will even add, more weariness, more care, more heart-ache than I know at this day. I may be singular in this confession, but I make it, and know it to be the truth. Since that dear hour when my soul cast itself on Jesus, I have found solid joy and peace; but before that, all those supposed gaieties of early youth, all the imagined ease and joy of boyhood, were but vanity and vexation of spirit to me. . That happy day, when I found the Saviour, and learned to cling to His dear feet, was a day never to be forgotten by me. An obscure child, unknown, unheard of, I listened to the Word of God; and that precious text led me to the cross of Christ. I can testify that the joy of that day was utterly indescribable. I could have leaped, I could have danced; there was no expression, however fanatical, which would have been out of keeping with the joy of my spirit at that hour. Many days of Christian experience have passed since then, but there has never been one which has had the full exhilaration, the sparkling delight which that first day had. I thought I could have sprung from the seat on which I sat, and have called out with the wildest of those Methodist brethren who were present, "I am forgiven! I am forgiven! A monument of grace! A sinner saved by blood! "My spirit saw its chains broken to pieces, I felt that I was an emancipated soul, an heir of Heaven, a forgiven one, accepted in Christ Jesus, plucked out of the miry clay and out of the horrible pit, with my feet set upon a rock, and my goings established. I thought I could dance all the way home. I could understand what John Bunyan meant, when he declared he wanted to tell the crows on the ploughed land all about his conversion. He was too full to hold, he felt he must tell somebody.

It is not everyone who can remember the very day and hour of his, deliverance; but, as Richard Knill said, "At such a time of the day, clang went every harp in Heaven, for Richard Knill was born again," it was e'en so with me.[2] The clock of mercy struck in Heaven the hour and moment of my emancipation, for the time had come. Between half-past ten o'clock, when I entered that chapel, and half-past twelve o'clock, when I was back again at home, what a change had taken place in me! I had passed from darkness into marvellous light, from death to life. Simply by looking to Jesus, I had been delivered from despair, and I was brought into such a joyous state of mind that, when they saw me at home, they said to me, "Something wonderful has happened to you;" and I was eager to tell them all about it. Oh! there was joy in the household that day, when all heard that the eldest son had found the Saviour, and knew himself to be forgiven,—bliss compared with which all earth's joys are less than nothing and vanity. Yes, I had looked to Jesus as I was, and found in Him my Saviour. Thus had the eternal purpose of Jehovah decreed it; and as, the moment before, there was none more wretched than I was, so, within that second, there was none more joyous. It took no longer time than does the lightning-flash; it was done, and never has it been undone. I looked, and lived, and leaped in joyful liberty as I beheld my sin punished upon the great Substitute, and put away for ever. I looked unto Him, as He bled upon that tree; His eyes darted a glance of love unutterable into my spirit, and in a moment, I was saved.[3] Looking unto Him, the bruises that my soul had suffered were healed, the gaping wounds were cured, the broken bones rejoiced, the rags that had covered me were all removed, my spirit was white as the spotless snows of the far-off North; I had melody within my spirit, for I was saved, washed, cleansed, forgiven, through Him that did hang upon the tree. My Master, I cannot understand how Thou couldst stoop Thine awful head to such a death as the death of the cross,—how Thou couldst take from Thy brow the coronet of stars which from old eternity had shone resplendent there; but how Thou shouldst permit the thorn-crown to gird Thy temples, astonishes me far more. That Thou shouldst cast away the mantle of Thy glory, the azure of Thine everlasting empire, I cannot comprehend: but how Thou shouldst have become veiled in the ignominious purple for a while, and then be mocked by impious men, who bowed to Thee as a pretended king; and how Thou shouldst be stripped naked to Thy shame, without a single covering, and die a felon's death;—this is still more incomprehensible. But the marvel is that Thou shouldst have suffered all this for *me!* Truly, Thy love to me is wonderful, passing the love of women! Was ever grief like Thine? Was ever love like Thine, that could open the flood-gates of such grief? Was ever love so mighty as to become the fount from which such an ocean of grief could come rolling down?

There was never anything so true to me as those bleeding hands, and that thorn-crowned head. Home, friends, health, wealth, comforts—all lost their lustre that day when He appeared, just as stars are hidden by the light of the sun. He was the only Lord and Giver of life's best bliss, the one well of living water springing up unto everlasting life. As I saw Jesus on His cross before me, and as

I mused upon His sufferings and death, methought I saw Him cast a look of love upon me; and then I looked at Him, and cried,—

> Jesu, lover of my soul,
> Let me to Thy bosom fly.'

He said, "Come," and I flew to Him, and clasped Him; and when He let me go again, I wondered where my burden was. It was gone! There, in the sepulchre, it lay, and I felt light as air; like a winged sylph, I could fly over mountains of trouble and despair; and oh! what liberty and joy I had! I could leap with ecstasy, for I had much forgiven, and I was freed from sin. With the spouse in the Canticles, I could say, *"I found Him;* "I, a lad, found the Lord of glory; I, a slave to sin, found the great Deliverer; I, the child of darkness, found the Light of life; I, the uttermost of the lost, found my Saviour and my God; I, widowed and desolate, found my Friend, my Beloved, my Husband. Oh, how I wondered that I should be pardoned! It was not the pardon that I wondered at so much; the wonder was that it should come to *me*. I marvelled that He should be able to pardon such sins as mine, such crimes, so numerous and so black; and that, after such an accusing conscience, He should have power to still every wave within my spirit, and make my soul like the surface of a river, undisturbed, quiet, and at ease. It mattered not to me whether the day itself was gloomy or bright, I had found Christ; that was enough for me. He was my Saviour, He was my all; and I can heartily say, that one day of pardoned sin was a sufficient recompense for the whole five years of conviction. I have to bless God for every terror that ever scared me by night, and for every foreboding that alarmed me by day. It has made me happier ever since; for now, if there be a trouble weighing upon my soul, I thank God it is not such a burden as that which bowed me to the very earth, and made me creep upon the ground, like a beast, by reason of heavy distress and affliction. I know I never can again suffer what I have suffered; I never can, except I be sent to hell, know more of agony than I have known; and now, that ease, that joy and peace in believing, that "no condemnation" which belongs to me as a child of God, is made doubly sweet and inexpressibly precious, by the recollection of my past days of sorrow and grief. Blessed be Thou, O God, for ever, who by those black days, like a dreary winter, bast made these summer days all the fairer and the sweeter! I need not walk through the earth fearful of every shadow, and afraid of every man I meet, for sin is washed away; my spirit is no more guilty; it is pure, it is holy. The frown of God no longer resteth upon me; but my Father smiles, I see His eyes,—they are glancing love; I hear His voice,—it is full of sweetness. I am forgiven, I am forgiven, I am forgiven!

When I look back upon it, I can see one reason why the Word was blessed to me as I heard it preached in that Primitive Methodist Chapel at Colchester; I had been up betimes crying to God for the blessing. As a lad, when I was seeking the Saviour, I used to rise with the sun, that I might get time to read gracious books, and to seek the Lord. I can recall the kind of pleas I used when I took my arguments, and came before the throne of grace: "Lord, save me; it will glorify Thy grace to save such a sinner as I am! Lord, save me, else I am lost to all eternity; do not let me perish, Lord! Save me, O Lord, for Jesus died! By His agony and bloody sweat, by His cross and passion, save me!" I often proved that the early morning was the best part of the day; I liked those prayers of which the psalmist said, "In the morning shall my prayer prevent Thee."

The Holy Spirit, who enabled me to believe, gave me peace through believing. I felt as sure that I was forgiven as before I felt sure of condemnation. I had been certain of my condemnation because the Word of God declared it, and my conscience bore witness to it; but when the Lord justified me, I was made equally certain by the same witnesses. The Word of the Lord in the Scripture saith, "He that believeth on Him is not condemned," and my conscience bore witness that I believed, and that God in pardoning me was just. Thus I had the witness of the Holy Spirit and also of my own conscience, and these two agreed in one. That great and excellent man, Dr. Johnson, used to hold the opinion that no man ever could know that he was pardoned,—that there was no such thing as assurance of faith. Perhaps, if Dr. Johnson had studied his Bible a little more, and had had a little more of the enlightenment of the Spirit, he, too, might have come to know his own pardon. Certainly, he was no very reliable judge of theology, any more than he was of porcelain, which he once attempted to make, and never succeeded. I think both in theology and porcelain his opinion is of very little value.

How can a man know that he is pardoned? There is a text which says, "Believe on the Lord Jesus Christ, and thou shalt be saved." I believe on the Lord Jesus Christ; is it irrational to believe that I am saved? "He that believeth on the Son hath everlasting life," saith Christ, in John's Gospel. I believe on Christ; am I absurd in believing that I have eternal life? I find the apostle Paul speaking by the Holy Ghost, and saying, "There is therefore now no condemnation to them that are in Christ Jesus. Being justified by faith, we have peace with God." If I know that my trust is fixed on Jesus only, and that I have faith in Him, were it not ten thousand times more absurd for me not to be at peace, than for me to be filled with joy unspeakable? It is but taking God at His Word, when the soul knows, as a necessary consequence of its faith, that it is saved. I took Jesus as my Saviour, and I was saved; and I can tell the reason why I took Him for my Saviour. To my own humiliation, I must confess that I did it because I could not help it; I was shut up to it. That stern law-work had hammered me into such a condition that, if there had been fifty other saviours, I could not have thought of them,—I was driven to this One. I wanted a Divine Saviour, I wanted One who was made a curse for me, to expiate my guilt. I wanted One who had died, for I deserved to die. I wanted One who had risen again, who was able by His life to make me live. I wanted the exact Saviour that stood before me in the Word, revealed to my heart; and I could not help having Him. I could realize then the language of Rutherford when, being full of love to Christ, once upon a time, in the dungeon of Aberdeen, he said, "O my Lord, if there were a broad hell betwixt me and Thee, if I could not get at Thee except by wading through it, I would not think twice, but I would go through it all, if I might but embrace Thee, and call Thee mine!" Oh, how I loved Him! Passing all loves except His own, was that love which I felt for Him then. If, beside the door of the place in which I met with Him, there had been a stake of blazing faggots, I would have stood upon them without chains, glad to give my flesh, and blood, and bones, to be ashes that should testify my love to Him. Had He asked me then to give all my substance to the poor, I would have given all, and thought myself to be amazingly rich in having beggared myself for His name's sake. Had He commanded me then to preach in the midst of all His foes, I could have said,—

"There's not a lamb in all Thy flock
I would disdain to feed,
There's not a foe, before whose face
I'd fear Thy cause to plead."

Has Jesus saved *me?* I dare not speak with any hesitation here;
I *know* He has. His Word is true, therefore I *am* saved. My evidence
that I am saved doe! not lie in the fact that I preach, or that I do
this or that. All my hope lies in this that Jesus Christ came to save
sinners. I am a sinner, I trust Him, then He cam, to save me, and
I am saved; I live habitually in the enjoyment of this blessed fact
and it is long since I have doubted the truth of it, for I have His
own Word to sustain my faith. It is a very surprising thing,—a thing
to be marvelled at most of all by those who enjoy it. I know that
it is to me even to this day the greatest wonder that I ever heard
of, that God should ever justify *me*. I feel myself to be a lump
of unworthiness, a mass of corruption, and a heap of sin apart
from His almighty love; yet I know, by a full assurance, that I am
justified by faith which is in Christ Jesus, and treated as if I had
been perfectly just, and made an heir of God and a joint-heir with
Christ; though by nature I must take my place among the most
sinful. I, who am altogether undeserving, am treated as if I had
been deserving. I am loved with as much love as if I had always
been godly, whereas aforetime I was ungodly.

I have always considered, with Luther and Calvin, that the
sum and substance of the gospel lies in that word *Substitution*,—
Christ standing in the stead of man. If I understand the gospel, it
is this: I deserve to be lost for ever; the only reason why I should
not be damned is, that Christ was punished in my stead, and there
is no need to execute a sentence twice for sin. On the other hand, I
know I cannot enter Heaven unless I have a perfect righteousness;
I am absolutely certain I shall never have one of my own, for I find
I sin every day; but then Christ had a perfect righteousness, and He
said, "There, poor sinner, take My garment, and put it on; you shall
stand before God as if you were Christ, and I will stand before God
as if I had been the sinner; I will suffer in the sinner's stead, and
you shall be rewarded for works which you did not do, but which I
did for you." I find it very convenient every day to come to Christ
as a sinner, as I came at the first. "You are no saint," says the devil.

Well, if I am not, I am a sinner, and Jesus Christ came into the world to save sinners. Sink or swim, I go to Him; other hope I have none. By looking to Him, I received all the faith which inspired me with confidence in His grace; and the word that first drew my soul—"Look unto Me,"—still rings its clarion note in my ears. There I once found conversion, and there I shall ever find refreshing and renewal.

Let me bear my personal testimony of what I have seen, what my own ears have heard, and my own heart has tasted. First, Christ is the only-begotten of the Father. He is Divine to me, if He be human to all the world besides. He has done that for me which none but a God could do. He has subdued my stubborn will, melted a heart of adamant, broken a chain of steel, opened the gates of brass, and snapped the bars of iron. He hath turned for me my mourning into laughter, and my desolation into joy; He hath led my captivity captive, and made my heart rejoice with joy unspeakable, and full of glory. Let others think as they will of Him, to me He must ever be the only-begotten of the Father: blessed be His holy name!

> Oh, that I could now adore Him,
> Like the Heavenly host above,
> Who for ever bow before Him,
> And unceasing sing His love!
> Happy songsters!
> When shall I your chorus join?

Again, I bear my testimony that He is full of grace. Ah, had He not been, I should never have beheld His glory. I was full of sin to overflowing. I was condemned already, because I believed not upon Him. He drew me when I wanted not to come, and though I struggled hard, He continued still to draw; and when at last I came to His mercy-seat, all trembling like a condemned culprit, He said, "Thy sins, which are many, are all forgiven thee: be of good cheer." Let others despise Him; but I bear witness that He is full of grace.

Finally, I bear my witness that He is full of truth. True have His promises been; not one has failed. I have often doubted Him, for that I blush; He has never failed me, in this I must rejoice. His promises have been yea and amen. I do but speak the testimony of every believer in Christ, though I put it thus personally to make it the more forcible. I bear witness that never servant had such a

Master as I have; never brother had such a Kinsman as He has been to me; never spouse had such a Husband as Christ has been to my soul; never sinner a better Saviour; never soldier a better Captain; never mourner a better Comforter than Christ bath been to my spirit. I want none beside Him. In life, He is my life; and in death, He shall be the death of death; in poverty, Christ is my riches; in sickness, He makes my bed; in darkness, He is my Star; and in brightness, He is my Sun. By faith I understand that the blessed Son of God redeemed my soul with His own heart's blood; and by sweet experience I know that He raised me up from the pit of dark despair, and set my feet on the rock. He died for me. This is the root of every satisfaction I have. He put all my transgressions away. He cleansed me with His precious blood; He covered me with His perfect righteousness; He wrapped me up in His own virtues. He has promised to keep me, while I abide in this world, from its temptations and snares; and when I depart from this world, He has already prepared for me a mansion in the Heaven of unfading bliss, and a crown of everlasting joy that shall never, never fade away. To me, then, the days or years of my mortal sojourn on this earth are of little moment. Nor is the manner of my decease of much consequence. Should foemen sentence me to martyrdom, or physicians declare that I must soon depart this life, it is all alike,—

> A few more rolling suns at most
> Shall land me on fair Canaan's coast."

What more can I wish than that, while my brief term on earth shall last, I should be the servant of Him who became the Servant of servants for me? I can say, concerning Christ's religion, if I had to die like a dog, and had no hope whatever of immortality, if I wanted to lead a happy life, let me serve my God with all my heart; let me be a follower of Jesus, and walk in His footsteps. If there were no hereafter, I would still prefer to be a Christian, and the humblest Christian minister, to being a king or an emperor, for I am persuaded there are more delights in Christ, yea, more joy in one glimpse of His face than is to be found in all the praises of this harlot-world, and in all the delights which it can yield to us in its sunniest and brightest days. And I am persuaded that what He has been till now, He will be. to the end; and where He bath begun a good work, He will carry it on. In the religion of Jesus Christ, there are clusters even on earth too heavy for one man to carry; there are fruits that have been found so rich that even angel lips have never been sweetened with more luscious wine; there are joys to be had here so fair that even cates ambrosial and the nectared wine of Paradise can scarcely excel the sweets of satisfaction that are to be found in the earthly banquets of the Lord. I have seen hundreds and thousands who have given their hearts to Jesus, but I never did see one who said he was disappointed with Him, I never met with one who said Jesus Christ was less than He was declared to be. When first my eyes beheld Him, when the burden slipped from off my heavy-laden shoulders, and I was free from condemnation, I thought that all the preachers I had ever heard had not half preached, they had not told half the beauty of my Lord and Master. So good! so generous! so gracious! so willing to forgive! It seemed to me as if they had almost slandered Him; they painted His likeness, doubtless, as well as they could, but it was a mere smudge compared with the matchless beauties of His face. All who have ever seen Him will say the same. I go back to my home, many a time, mourning that I cannot preach my Master even as I myself know Him, and what I know of Him is very little compared with the matchlessness of His grace. Would that I knew more of Him, and that I could tell it out better!

* * * * *

1   It is remarkable that no less than three persons claimed to have been the preacher on this occasion, but Mr. Spurgeon did not recognize any one of them as the man to whom he then listened.

2   It is definitely known that the date of Mr. Spurgeon's conversion was January 6th, 1850, for preaching at New Park Street Chapel, on Lord's-day morning, January 6th, 1856, from Isaiah 45:22, he said that, six years before, that very day, and at that very hour, he had been led to look to Christ, by a sermon from that text.

3   On one of the foundation stones of the School-Chapel erected at Bexhill-on-Sea in ever-loving memory of Mr. Spurgeon, the following inscription has been cut, in the hope that passersby may find salvation through reading the passage of Scripture which was blessed to his conversion:—

HOW C. H. SPURGEON FOUND CHRIST.
I looked to Him;
He looked on me;
And we were one for ever."—C. H. S.

Look unto Me, and be ye Saved, all the ends of the earth; for I am God, and there is none else."—Isaiah 45:22.

THE GREATEST FIGHT IN THE WORLD

ALTHOUGH one of the smallest of the Spurgeon volumes, this is among the most notable of his publications. It consists of the inaugural address which he delivered at the Pastor's College Conference in April 1891. Taking "the good fight of faith" as his theme, he exhorted his audience to do their very best "in our great Master's service."

Published just before his death, this volume constitutes Spurgeon's final address to his fellow pastors. Without a doubt it is one of the most forceful addresses that he ever delivered.

"Fight the good fight of faith"—1 Timothy 6:12.

Introduction

May all the prayers which have already been offered up be answered abundantly and speedily! May more of such pleading follow that in which we have united! The most memorable part of past Conferences has been the holy concert of believing prayer; and I trust we are not falling off in that respect, but growing yet more fervent and prevalent in intercession. On his knees the believer is invincible.

I am greatly concerned about this Address for many months before it comes on: assuredly it is to me the child of many prayers. I should like to be able to speak well on so worthy an occasion, wherein the best of speech may well be enlisted; but I desire to be, as our brother's prayer has put it, absolutely in the Lord's hands, in this matter as well as in every other. I would be willing to speak with stammering tongue if God's purpose could so be answered more fully; and I would even gladly lose all power of speech if, by being famished as to human words, you might feed the better on that spiritual meat which is to be found alone in Him, who is the incarnate Word of God.

I may say to you, as speakers, that I am persuaded we should prepare ourselves with diligence, and try to do our very best in our great Master's service. I think I have read that when a handful of lion-like Greeks held the pass against the Persians, a spy, who came to see what they were doing, went back and told the great king that they were poor creatures, for they were busied in combing their hair. The despot saw things in a true light when the learned that a people who could adjust their hair before battle had set a great value on their heads, and would not bow them to a coward's death. If we are very careful to use our best language when proclaiming eternal truths, we may leave our opponents to infer that we are still more careful of the doctrines themselves. We must not be untidy soldiers when a great fight is before us, for that would look like despondency. Into the battle against false doctrine, and worldliness, and sin, we advance without a fear as to the ultimate issue; and therefore our talk should not be that of ragged passion, but of well-considered principle. It is not ours to be slovenly, since we look to be triumphant. Do you work well at this time, that all men may see that you are not going to be driven from it. The Persian said, when on another occasion he saw a handful of warriors advancing, "That little handful of men! Surely, they cannot mean fighting!" But one who stood by said, "Yes, they do, for they have burnished their shields, and brightened their armour." Men mean business, depend upon it, when they are not to be hurried into disorder. It was the way amongst the Greeks, when they had a bloody day before them, to show the stern joy of warriors by being well adorned. I think, brethren, that when we have great work to do for Christ, and mean doing it, we shall not go to the pulpit or the platform to say the first thing that comes to the lip. If we speak for Jesus we ought to speak at our best, though, even then, men are not killed by the glitter of shields, nor by the smoothness of a warrior's hair; but a higher power is needed to cut through coats of mail. To the God of armies I look up. May He defend the right! But with no careless step do I advance to the front; neither does any doubt possess me. We are feeble, but the Lord our God is mighty, and the battle is the Lord's, rather than ours.

Only one fear is upon me to a certain degree. I am anxious that my deep sense of responsibility may not lessen my efficiency. A man may feel that he ought to do so well that, for that very reason, he may not do as well as he might. An overpowering feeling of responsibility may breed paralysis. I once recommended a young clerk to a bank, and his friends very properly gave him strict charge to be very careful in his figures. This advice he heard times out of mind. He became so extremely careful as to grow nervous, and whereas he had been accurate before, his anxiety caused him to make blunder after blunder, till he left his situation. It is possible to be so anxious as to how and what you shall speak, that your manner grows constrained, and you forget those very points which you meant to make most prominent.

Brethren, I am telling some of my private thoughts to you, because we are alike in our calling; and having the same experiences, it does us good to know that it is so. We who lead have the same weaknesses and troubles as you who follow. We must prepare, but we must also trust in Him without whom nothing begins, continues, or ends aright.

I have this comfort, that even if I should not speak adequately upon my theme, the topic itself will speak to you. There is something even in starting an appropriate subject. If a man speaks well upon a subject which has no practical importance, it is not well that he should have spoken. As one of the ancients said, "It is idle to speak much to the point upon a matter which itself is not to the point." Carve a cherry-stone with the utmost skill, and at best it is but a cherry-stone; while a diamond if badly cut is still a precious stone. If the matter be of great weight, even if the man cannot speak up to his theme, yet to call attention to it is no vain thing. The subjects which we shall consider at this time ought to be considered, and to be considered just now. I have chosen present and pressing truths, and if you will think them out for yourselves, you will not lose the time occupied by this address. With what inward fervour do I pray that we may all be profited by this hour of meditation!

Happily the themes are such that I can exemplify them even in this address. As a smith can teach his apprentice *while* making a horseshoe; yes, and *by* making a horseshoe; so can we make our own sermons examples of the doctrine they contain. In this case we can practise what we preach, if the Lord be with us. A lecturer in cookery instructs his pupils by following his own recipes. He prepares a dish before his audience, and while he describes the viands and their preparation, he tastes the food himself, and his friends are refreshed also. He will succeed by his dainty dishes, even if he is not a man of eloquent speech. The man who feeds is surer of success than he who only plays well upon an instrument, and leaves with his audience no memory but that of pleasant sound. If the subjects which we bring before our people are in themselves good, they will make up for our want of skill in setting them forth. So long as the guests get the spiritual meat, the servitor at the table may be happy to be forgotten.

My topics have to do with our life-work, with the crusade against error and sin in which we are engaged. I hope that every man here wears the red cross on his heart, and is pledged to do and dare for Christ and for his cross, and never to be satisfied till Christ's foes are routed and Christ himself is satisfied. Our fathers used to speak of "The Cause of God and Truth"; and it is for this that we bear arms, the few against the many, the feeble against the mighty. Oh, to be found good soldiers of Jesus Christ!

Three things are of the utmost importance just now, and, indeed, they always have stood, and always will stand in the front rank for practical purposes. The first is *our armoury,* which is the inspired Word; the second is *our army,* the church of the living God, called out by himself, which we must lead under our Lord's command; and the third is *our strength,* by which we wear the armour and wield the sword. The Holy Spirit is our power to be and to do; to suffer and to serve; to grow and to fight; to wrestle and to overcome. Our third theme is of main importance, and though we place it last, we rank it first.

Our Armoury

WE WILL begin with OUR ARMOURY. That armoury is to me, at any rate—and I hope it is to each one of you—THE BIBLE. To us Holy Scripture is as "the tower of David builded for an armoury, whereon there hang a thousand bucklers, all shields of mighty men." If we want weapons we must come here for them, and here only. Whether we seek the sword of offence or the shield of defence, we must find it within the volume of inspiration. If others have any other storehouse, I confess at once I have none. I have nothing else to preach when I have got through with this book. Indeed, I can have no wish to preach at all if I may not continue to expound the subjects which I find in these pages. What else is worth preaching? Brethren, the truth of God is the only treasure for which we seek, and the Scripture is the only field in which we dig for it.

We need nothing more than God has seen fit to reveal. Certain errant spirits are never at home till they are abroad: they crave for a something which I think they will never find, either in heaven above, or in the earth beneath, or in the water under the earth, so long as they are in their present mind. They never rest, for they will have nothing to do with an infallible revelation; and hence they are doomed to wander throughout time and eternity, and find no abiding city. For the moment they glory as if they were satisfied with their last new toy; but in a few months it is sport to them to break in pieces all the notions which they formerly prepared with care, and paraded with delight. They go up a hill only to come down again. Indeed, they say that the pursuit of truth is better than truth itself. They like fishing better than the fish; which may very well be true, since their fish are very small, and very full of bones. These men are as great at destroying their own theories as certain paupers are at tearing up their clothes. They begin again *de novo,* times without number: their house is always having its foundation digged out. They should be good at beginnings; for they have always been beginning since we have known them. They are as the rolling thing before the whirlwind, or "like the troubled sea, when it cannot rest, whose waters cast up mire and dirt." Although their cloud is not that cloud which betokened the divine presence, yet it is always moving before them, and their tents are scarcely pitched before it is time for the stakes to be pulled up again. These men are not even seeking certainty; their heaven lies in shunning all fixed truth, and following every will-o'-the-wisp of speculation: they are ever learning, but they never come to the knowledge of the truth.

As for us, we cast anchor in the haven of the Word of God. Here is our peace, our strength, our life, our motive, our hope, our happiness. God's Word is our ultimatum. Here we have it. Our understanding cries, "I have found it"; our conscience asserts that here is *the truth;* and our heart finds here a support to which all her affections can cling; and hence we rest content.

If the revelation of God were not enough for our faith, what could we add to it? Who can answer this question? What would any man propose to add to the sacred Word? A moment's thought would lead us to scout with derision the most attractive words of men, if it were proposed to add them to the Word of God. The fabric would not be of a piece. Would you add rags to a royal vestment? Would you pile the filth of the streets in a king's treasury? Would you join the pebbles of the sea-shore to the diamonds of Golconda? Anything more than the Word of God sets before us, for us to believe and to preach as the life of men, seems utterly absurd to us; yet we confront a generation of men who are always wanting to discover a new motive power, and a new gospel for their churches. The coverlet of their bed does not seem to be long enough, and they would fain borrow a yard or two of linsey-woolsey from the Unitarian, the Agnostic, or even the Atheist. Well; if there be any spiritual force or heavenward power to be found beyond that reported of in this Book, I think we can do without it: indeed, it must be such a sham that we are better without it. The Scriptures in their own sphere are like God in the universe—All-sufficient. In them is revealed all the light and power the mind of man can need in spiritual things. We hear of other motive power beyond that which lies in the Scriptures, but we believe such a force to be a pretentious nothing. A train is off the lines, or otherwise unable to proceed, and a break-down gang has arrived. Engines are brought to move the great impediment. At first there seems to be no stir: the engine power is not enough. Harken! A small boy has it. He cries, "Father, if they have not power enough, I will lend them my rocking-horse to help them." We have had the offer of a considerable number of rocking-horses of late. They have not accomplished much that I can see, but they promised fair. I fear their effect has been for evil rather than good: they have moved the people to derision, and have driven them out of the places of worship which once they were glad to crowd. The new toys have been exhibited, and the people, after seeing them for a little, have moved on to other toy-shops. These fine new nothings have done no good, and they never will do any good while the world standeth. The Word of God is quite sufficient to interest and bless the souls of men throughout all time; but novelties soon fail. "Surely," cries one, "we must add our own thoughts thereto." My brother, think by all means; but the thoughts of God are better than yours. You may shed fine thoughts, as trees in autumn cast their leaves; but there is One who knows more about your thoughts than you do, and he thinks little of them. Is it not written, "The Lord knoweth the thoughts of man, that they are vanity"? To liken *our* thoughts to the great thoughts of God, would be a gross absurdity. Would you bring your candle to show the sun? Your nothingness to replenish the eternal all? It is better to be silent before the Lord, than to dream of supplementing what he has spoken. The Word of the Lord is to the conceptions of men as a garden to a wilderness. Keep within the covers of the sacred book, and you are in the land which floweth with milk and honey; why seek to add to it the desert sands?

Try not to cast anything forth from the perfect volume. If you find it there, there let it stand, and be it yours to preach it according to the analogy and proportion of faith. That which is worthy of God's revealing is worthy of our preaching; and that is all too little for me to claim for it. "By every word of the Lord doth man live." "Every word of God is pure: he is a shield unto them that put their trust in him." Let every revealed truth be brought forth in its own season. Go not elsewhere for a subject: with such infinity before you, there can be no need that you should do so; with such glorious truth to preach, it will be wanton wickedness if you do.

The adaption of all this provision for our warfare we have already tested: the weapons of our armoury are the very best; for we have made trial of them, and have found them so. Some of you, younger brethren, have only tested the Scripture a little as yet; but others of us, who are now getting grey, can assure you that we have tried the Word, as silver is tried in a furnace of earth; and it has stood every test, even unto seventy times seven. The sacred Word has endured more criticism than the best accepted form of philosophy or science, and it has survived every ordeal. As a living divine has said, "After its present assailants are all dead, their funeral sermons will be preached from this Book—not one verse omitted—from the first page of Genesis to the last page of Revelation." Some of us have lived for many years, in daily conflict, perpetually putting to the proof the Word of God; and we can honestly give you this assurance, that it is equal to every emergency. After using this sword of two edges upon coats of mail, and bucklers of brass, we find no notch in its edge. It is neither broken nor blunted in the fray. It would cleave the devil himself, from the crown of his head to the sole of his foot; and yet it would show no sign of failure whatsoever. Today it is still the self-same mighty Word of God that it was in the hands of our Lord Jesus. How it strengthens us when we remember the many conquests of souls which we have achieved through the sword of the Spirit! Have any of you known or heard of such a thing as conversion wrought by any other doctrine than that which is in the Word? I should like to have a catalogue of conversions wrought by modern theology. I would subscribe for a copy of such a work. I will not say what I might do with it after I had read it; but I would, at least, increase its sale by one copy, just to see what progressive divinity pretends to have done. Conversions through the doctrines of universal restitution! Conversions through the doctrines of doubtful inspiration! Conversions to the love of God, and to faith in his Christ, by hearing that the death of the Saviour was only the consummation of a grand example, but not a substitutionary sacrifice! Conversions by a gospel out of which all the gospel has been drained! They say, "Wonders will never cease"; but such wonders will never begin. Let them report changes of heart so wrought, and give us an opportunity of testing them; and then, perchance, we may consider whether it is worth our while to leave that Word which we have tried in hundreds, and, some of us here, in many thousands of cases, and have always found effectual for salvation. We know why they sneer at conversions. These are grapes which such foxes cannot reach, and therefore they are sour. As we believe in the new birth, and expect to see it in thousands of cases, we shall adhere to that Word of truth by which the Holy Spirit works regeneration. In a word, in our warfare we shall keep to the old weapon of the sword of the Spirit, until we can find a better. "There is none like that; give it me", is at present our verdict.

How often we have seen the Word made effectual for consolation! It is, as one brother expressed it in prayer, a difficult thing to deal with broken hearts. What a fool I have felt myself to be when trying to bring forth a prisoner out of Giant Despair's Castle! How hard it is to persuade despondency to hope! How have

I tried to trap my game by every art known to me; but when almost in my grasp the creature has burrowed another hole! I had dug him out of twenty already, and then have had to begin again. The convicted sinner uses all kinds of arguments to prove that he cannot be saved. The inventions of despair are as many as the devices of self-confidence. There is no letting light into the dark cellar of doubt, except through the window of the Word of God. Within the Scripture there is a balm for every wound, a salve for every sore. Oh, the wondrous power in the Scripture to create a soul of hope within the ribs of despair, and bring eternal light into the darkness which has made a long midnight in the inmost soul! Often have we tried the Word of the Lord as "the cup of consolation", and it has never failed to cheer the despondent. We know what we say, for we have witnessed the blessed facts: the Scriptures of truth, applied by the Holy Spirit, have brought peace and joy to those who sat in darkness and in the valley of the shadow of death.

We have also observed the excellence of the Word in the edification of believers, and in the production of righteousness, holiness, and usefulness. We are always being told, in these days, of the "ethical" side of the gospel. I pity those to whom this is a novelty. Have they not discovered this before? We have always been dealing with the ethical side of the gospel; indeed, we find it ethical all over. There is no true doctrine which has not been fruitful in good works. Payson wisely said, "If there is one fact, one doctrine, or promise in the Bible, which has produced no practical effect upon your temper or conduct, be assured that you do not truly believe it." All Scriptural teaching has its practical purpose, and its practical result; and what we have to say, not as a matter of discovery, but as a matter of plain common sense, is this, that if we have had fewer fruits than we could wish *with* the tree, we suspect that there will be no fruit at all when the tree has gone, and the roots are dug up. The very root of holiness lies in the gospel of our Lord Jesus Christ; and if this be removed with a view to more fruitfulness, the most astounding folly will have been committed. We have seen a fine morality, a stern integrity, a delicate purity, and, what is more, a devout holiness, produced by the doctrines of grace. We see consecration in life, we see calm resignation in the hour of suffering, we see joyful confidence in the article of death, and these, not in a few instances, but as the general outcome of intelligent faith in the teachings of Scripture. We have even wondered at the sacred result of the old gospel. Though we are accustomed often-times to see it, it never loses its charm. We have seen poor men and women yielding themselves to Christ, and living for him, in a way that has made our hearts to bow in adoration of the God of grace. We have said, "This must be a true gospel which can produce such lives as these." If we have not talked so much about ethics as some have done, we remember an old saying of the country folk: "Go to such a place to hear about good works, but go to another place to see them." Much talk, little work. Great cry is the token of little wool. Some have preached good works till there has scarcely been left a decent person in the parish; while others have preached free grace and dying love in such a way that sinners have become saints, and saints have been as boughs loaded down with fruit to the praise and glory of God. Having seen the harvest which springs from our seed, we are not going to change it at the dictates of this whimsical age.

Especially we have seen and tested the efficacy of the Word of God when we have been by the sick bed. I was, but a few days ago, by the side of one of our elders, who appeared to be dying; and it was like heaven below to converse with him. I never saw so much joy at a wedding as I saw in that quiet chamber. He hoped soon to be with Jesus; and he was joyful in the prospect. He said, "I have no doubt, no cloud, no trouble, no want; nay, I have not even a wish. The doctrine you have taught has served me to live by, and now it serves me to die by. I am resting upon the precious blood of Christ, and it is a firm foundation." And he added, "How silly all those letters against the gospel now appear to me! I have read some of them, and I have noted the attacks upon the old faith, but they seem quite absurd to me now that I lie on the verge of eternity. What could the new doctrine do for me now?" I came down from my interview greatly strengthened and gladdened by the good man's testimony; and all the more was I personally comforted because it was the Word which I myself had constantly preached which had been such a blessing to my friend. If God had so owned it from so poor an instrument, I felt that the Word itself must be good indeed. I am never so happy amidst all the shouts of youthful merriment as on the day when I hear the dying testimony of one who is resting on the everlasting gospel of the grace of God. The ultimate issue, as seen upon a dying-bed, is a true test, as it is an inevitable one. Preach that which will enable men to face death without fear, and you will preach nothing but the old gospel.

Brethren, we will array ourselves in that which God has supplied us in the armoury of inspired Scripture, because every weapon in it has been tried and proved in many ways; and never has any part of our panoply failed us.

Moreover, we shall evermore keep to the Word of God, because *we have had experience of its power within ourselves.* It is not so long ago that you will have forgotten how, like a hammer, the Word of God broke your flinty heart, and brought down your stubborn will. By the Word of the Lord you were brought to the cross, and comforted by the atonement. That Word breathed a new life into you; and when, for the first time, you knew yourself to be a child of God, you felt the ennobling power of the gospel received by faith. The Holy Spirit wrought your salvation through the Holy Scriptures. You trace your conversion, I am sure, to the Word of the Lord; for this alone is "perfect, converting the soul." Whoever may have been the man who spoke it, or whatever may have been the book in which you read it, it was not man's Word, nor man's thought upon God's Word, but the Word itself, which made you know salvation in the Lord Jesus. It was neither human reasoning, nor the force of eloquence, nor the power of moral suasion, but the omnipotence of the Spirit, applying the Word itself, that gave you rest and peace and joy through believing. We are ourselves trophies of the power of the sword of the Spirit; he leads us in triumph in every place, the willing captives of his grace. Let no man marvel that we keep close to it.

How many times since conversion has Holy Scripture been everything to you! You have your fainting fits, I suppose: have you not been restored by the precious cordial of the promise of the Faithful One? A passage of Scripture laid home to the heart speedily quickens the feeble heart into mighty action. Men speak of waters that revive the spirits, and tonics that brace the constitution; but the Word of God has been more than this to us, times beyond count. Amidst temptations sharp and strong, and trials fierce and bitter, the Word of the Lord has preserved us. Amidst discouragements which damped our hopes, and disappointments which wounded our hearts, we have felt ourselves strong to do and bear, because the assurances of help which we find in our Bibles have brought us a secret, unconquerable energy.

Brethren, we have had experience of the elevation which the Word of God can give us—upliftings towards God and heaven. If you get studying books contrary to the inspired volume, are you not conscious of slipping downwards? I have known some to whom such reading has been as a mephitic vapour surrounding them with the death-damp. Yes; and I may add, that to forego your Bible reading for the perusal even of good books would soon bring a conscious descending of the soul. Have you not found that even gracious books may be to you as a plain to look down upon, rather than as a summit to which to aspire? You have come up to their level long ago, and get no higher by reading them: it is idle to spend precious time upon them. Was it ever so with you and the Book of God? Did you ever rise above its simplest teaching, and feel that it tended to draw you downward? Never! In proportion as your mind becomes saturated with Holy Scripture, you are conscious of being lifted right up, and carried aloft as on eagles' wings. You seldom come down from a solitary Bible reading without feeling that you have drawn near to God: I say a solitary one; for when reading with others, the danger is that stale comments may be flies in the pot of ointment. The prayerful study of the Word is not only a means of instruction, but an act of devotion wherein the transforming power of grace is often exercised, changing us into the image of him of whom the Word is a mirror. Is there anything, after all, like the Word of God when the open books finds open hearts? When I read the lives of such men as Baxter, Brainerd, McCheyne, and many others, why, I feel like one who has bathed himself in some cool brook after having gone a journey through a black country, which left him dusty and depressed; and this result comes of the fact that such men embodied Scripture in their lives and illustrated it in their experience. The washing of water by the Word is what they had, and what we need. We must get it where they found it. To see the effects of the truth of God in the lives of holy men is confirmatory to faith and stimulating to holy aspiration. Other influences do not help us to such a sublime ideal of consecration. If you read the Babylonian books of the present day, you will catch their spirit, and it is a foreign one, which will draw you aside from the Lord your God. You may also get great harm from divines in whom there is much pretence of the Jerusalem dialect, but their speech is half of Ashdod: these will confuse your mind and defile your faith. It may chance that a book which is upon the whole excellent, which has little taint about it, may do you more mischief than a thoroughly bad one. Be careful; for works of this kind come forth from the press like clouds of locusts. Scarcely can you find in these days a book which is quite free from the modern leaven, and the least particle of it ferments till it produces the wildest error. In reading books of the new order, though no palpable falsehood may appear, you are conscious of a twist being given you, and of a sinking in the tone of your spirit; therefore be on your guard. But with your Bible you may always feel at ease; there every breath from every quarter brings life and health. If you keep close to the inspired book, you can suffer no harm; say rather you are at the fountain-head of all moral and spiritual good. This is fit food for men of God: this is the bread which nourishes the highest life.

After preaching the gospel for forty years, and after printing the sermons I have preached for more than six-and-thirty years, reaching now to the number of 2,200 in weekly succession, I am fairly entitled to speak about the fulness and richness of the Bible, as a preacher's book. Brethren, it is inexhaustible. No question about freshness will arise if we keep closely to the text of the sacred volume. There can be no difficulty as to finding themes totally distinct from those we have handled before; the variety is as infinite as the fulness. A long life will only suffice us to skirt the shores of this great continent of light. In the forty years of my own ministry I have only touched the hem of the garment of divine truth; but what virtue has flowed out of it! The Word is like its Author, infinite, immeasurable, without end. If you were ordained to be a preacher throughout eternity, you would have before you a theme equal to everlasting demands. Brothers, shall we each have a pulpit somewhere amidst the spheres? Shall we have a parish of millions of leagues? Shall we have voices so strengthened as to reach attentive constellations? Shall we be witnesses for the Lord of grace to myriads of worlds which will be wonder-struck when they hear of the incarnate God? Shall we be surrounded by pure intelligences enquiring and searching into the mystery of God manifest in the flesh? Will the unfallen worlds desire to be instructed in the glorious gospel of the blessed God? And will each one of us have his own tale to tell of our experience of infinite love? I think so, since the Lord has saved us "to the intent that now unto the principalities and powers in heavenly places might be known by the church of the manifold wisdom of God." If such be the case, our Bibles will suffice for ages to come for new themes every morning, and for fresh songs and discourses world without end.

We are resolved, then, since we have this arsenal supplied for us of the Lord, and since we want no other, to use the Word of God only, and *to use it with greater energy. We are resolved*—and I hope there is no dissentient among us—*to know our Bibles better.* Do we know the sacred volume half so well as we should know it? Have we laboured after as complete a knowledge of the Word of God as many a critic has obtained of his favourite classic? Is it not possible that we still meet with passages of Scripture which are new to us? Should it be so? Is there any part of what the Lord has written which you have never read? I was struck with my brother Archibald Brown's observation, that he bethought himself that unless he read the Scriptures through from end to end there might be inspired teachings which had never been known to him, and so he resolved to read the books in their order; and having done so once, he continued the habit. Have we, any of us, omitted to do this? Let us begin at once. I love to see how readily certain of our brethren turn up an appropriate passage, and then quote its fellow, and crown all with a third. They seem to know exactly the passage which strikes the nail on the head. They have their Bibles, not only in their hearts, but at their fingers' ends. This is a most valuable attainment for a minister. A good textuary is a good theologian. Certain others, whom I esteem for other things, are yet weak on this point, and seldom quote a text of Scripture correctly: indeed, their alterations jar on the ear of the Bible reader. It is sadly common among ministers to add a word or subtract a word from the passage, or in some way to debase the language of sacred writ. How often have I heard brethren speak about making "your calling and salvation" sure! Possibly they hardly enjoyed so much as we do the Calvinistic word "election", and therefore they allowed the meaning; nay, in some cases contradict it. Our reverence for the great Author of Scripture should forbid all mauling of his words. No alteration of Scripture can by any possibility be an improvement. Believers in verbal inspiration should be studiously careful to be verbally correct. The gentlemen who see errors in Scripture may think themselves competent to amend the language of the Lord of hosts; but we who believe God, and accept the very words he uses, may not make so presumptuous an attempt. Let us quote the words as they stand in the best possible translation, and it will be better still if we know the original, and can tell if our version fails to give the sense. How much mischief may arise out of an accidental alteration of the Word! Blessed are they who are in accord with the divine teaching, and receive its true meaning, as the Holy Ghost teaches them! Oh, that we might know the Spirit of Holy Scripture thoroughly, drinking it in, til we are saturated with it! This is the blessing which we resolve to obtain.

By God's grace we purpose to believe the Word of God more intensely. There is believing, and believing. You believe in all your brethren here assembled, but in some of them you have a conscious practical confidence, since in your hour of trouble they have come to your rescue and proved themselves brothers born for adversity. You confide in these, with absolute certitude, because you have personally tried them. Your faith was faith before; but now it is a higher, firmer, and more assured confidence. Believe in the inspired volume up to the hilt. Believe it right through; believe it thoroughly; believe it with the whole strength of your being. Let the truths of Scripture become the chief factors in your life, the chief operative forces of your action. Let the great transactions of the gospel story be to you as really and practically facts, as any fact which meets you in the domestic circle, or in the outside world: let them be as vividly true to you as your own ever present body, with its aches and pains, its appetites and joys. If we can get out of the realm of fiction and fancy, into the world of fact, we shall have struck a vein of power which will yield us countless treasure of strength. Thus, to become "mighty in the Scriptures" will be to become "mighty through God."

We should resolve also that we will quote more of Holy Scripture. Sermons should be full of Bible; sweetened, strengthened, sanctified with Bible essence. The kind of sermons that people need to hear are outgrowths of Scripture. If they do not love to hear them, there is all the more reason why they should be preached to them. The gospel has the singular faculty of creating a taste for itself. Bible hearers, when they hear indeed, come to be

Bible lovers. The mere stringing of texts together is a poor way of making sermons; though some have tried it, and I doubt not God has blessed them, since they did their best. It is far better to string texts together, than to pour out one's own poor thoughts in a washy flood. There will at least be something to be thought of and remembered if the Holy Word be quoted; and in the other case there may be nothing whatever. Texts of Scripture need not, however, be strung together, they may be fitly brought in to give edge and point to a discourse. They will be the force of the sermon. Our own words are mere paper pellets compared with the rifle shot of the Word. The Scripture is the conclusion of the whole matter. There is no arguing after we find that "It is written." To a large extent in the hearts and consciences of our hearers debate is over when the Lord has spoken. "Thus saith the Lord" is the end of discussion to Christian minds; and even the ungodly cannot resist Scripture without resisting the Spirit who wrote it. That we may speak convincingly we will speak Scripturally.

We are further resolved that we will preach nothing but the Word of God. The alienation of the masses from hearing the gospel is largely to be accounted for by the sad fact that it is not always the gospel that they hear if they go to places of worship; and all else falls short of what their souls need. Have you never heard of a king who made a series of great feasts, and bade many, week after week? He had a number of servants who were appointed to wait at his table; and these went forth on the appointed days, and spake with the people. But, somehow, after a while the bulk of the people did not come to the feasts. They came in decreasing number; but the great mass of citizens turned their backs on the banquets. The king made enquiry, and he found that the food provided did not seem to satisfy the men who came to look upon the banquets; and so they came no more. He determined himself to examine the tables and the meats placed thereon. He saw much finery and many pieces of display which never came out of his storehouses. He looked at the food and he said, "But how is this? These dishes, how came they here? These are not of my providing. My oxen and fatlings were killed, yet we have not here the flesh of fed beasts, but hard meat from cattle lean and starved. Bones are here, but where is the fat and the marrow? The bread also is coarse; whereas mine was made of the finest wheat? The wine is mixed with water, and the water is not from a pure well." One of those who stood by answered and said, "O king, we thought that the people would be surfeited with marrow and fatness, and so we gave them bone and gristle to try their teeth upon. We thought also that they would be weary of the best white bread, and so we baked a little at our own homes, in which the bran and husks were allowed to remain. It is the opinion of the learned that our provision is more suitable for these times than that which your majesty prescribed so long ago. As for the wines on the lees, the taste of men runs not that way in this age; and so transparent a liquid as pure water is too light a draught for men who are wont to drink of the river of Egypt, which has a taste in it of mud from the Mountains of the Moon." Then the king knew why the people came not to the feast. Does the reason why going to the house of God has become so distasteful to a great many of the population, lie in this direction? I believe it does. Have our Lord's servants been chopping up their own odds and ends and tainted bits, to make therewith a potted meat for the millions; and do the millions therefore turn away? Listen to the rest of my parable. "Clear the tables!" cried the king in indignation: "Cast that rubbish to the dogs. Bring in the barons of beef: set forth my royal provender. Remove those gewgaws from the hall, and that adulterated bread from the table, and cast out the water of the muddy river." They did so; and if my parable is right, very soon there was a rumour throughout the streets that truly royal dainties were to be had, and the people thronged the palace, and the king's name became exceeding great throughout the land. Let us try the plan. May be, we shall soon rejoice to see our Master's banquet furnished with guests.

We are resolved, then, to use more fully than ever what God has provided for us in this Book, for *we are sure of its inspiration*. Let me say that over again. WE ARE SURE OF ITS INSPIRATION. You will notice that attacks are frequently made as against *verbal* inspiration. The form chosen is a mere pretext. Verbal inspiration is the verbal form of the assault, but the attack is really aimed at inspiration itself. You will not read far in the essay before you will find that the gentleman who started with contesting a theory of inspiration which none of us ever held, winds up by showing his hand, and that hand wages war with inspiration itself. There is the true point. We care little for any theory of inspiration: in fact, we have none. To us the plenary verbal inspiration of Holy Scripture is fact, and not hypothesis. It is a pity to theorize upon a subject which is deeply mysterious, and makes a demand upon faith rather than fancy. Believe in the inspiration of Scripture, and believe it in the most intense sense. You will not believe in a truer and fuller inspiration than really exists. No one is likely to err in that direction, even if error be possible. If you adopt theories which pare off a portion here, and deny authority to a passage there, you will at last have no inspiration left, worthy of the name.

If this book be not infallible, where shall we find infallibility? We have given up the Pope, for he has blundered often and terribly; but we shall not set up instead of him a horde of little popelings fresh from college. Are these correctors of Scripture infallible? Is it certain that our Bibles are not right, but that the critics must be so? The old silver is to be depreciated; but the German silver, which is put in its place, is to be taken at the value of gold. Striplings fresh from reading the last new novel correct the notions of their fathers, who were men of weight and character. Doctrines which produced the godliest generation that ever lived on the face of the earth are scouted as sheer folly. Nothing is so obnoxious to these creatures as that which has the smell of Puritanism upon it. Every little man's nose goes up celestially at the very sound of the word "Puritan"; though if the Puritans were here again, they would not dare to treat them thus cavalierly; for if Puritans did fight, they were soon known as Ironsides, and their leader could hardly be called a fool, even by those who stigmatized him as a "tyrant." Cromwell, and they that were with him, were not all weak-minded persons— surely? Strange that these are lauded to the skies by the very men who deride their true successors, believers in the same faith. But where shall infallibility be found? "The depth saith, it is not in me"; yet those who have no depth at all would have us imagine that it is in them; or else by perpetual change they hope to hit upon it. Are we now to believe that infallibility is with learned men? Now, Farmer Smith, when you have read your Bible, and have enjoyed its precious promises, you will have, tomorrow morning, to go down the street to ask the scholarly man at the parsonage whether this portion of the Scripture belongs to the inspired part of the Word, or whether it is of dubious authority. It will be well for you to know whether it was written by *the* Isaiah, or whether it was by the second of the "two Obadiahs." All possibility of certainty is transferred from the spiritual man to a class of persons whose scholarship is pretentious, but who do not even pretend to spirituality. We shall gradually be so bedoubted and becriticized, that only a few of the most profound will know what is Bible, and what is not, and they will dictate to all the rest of us. I have no more faith in their mercy than in their accuracy: they will rob us of all that we hold most dear, and glory in the cruel deed. This same reign of terror we shall not endure, for we still believe that God revealeth himself rather to babes than to the wise and prudent, and we are fully assured that our own old English version of the Scriptures is sufficient for plain men for all purposes of life, salvation, and godliness. We do not despise learning, but we will never say of culture or criticism. "These be thy gods, O Israel!"

Do you see why men would lower the degree of inspiration in Holy Writ, and would fain reduce it to an infinitesimal quantity? It is because the truth of God is to be supplanted. If you ever go into a shop in the evening to buy certain goods which depend so much upon colour and texture as to be best judged of by daylight; if, after you have got into the shop, the tradesman proceeds to lower the gas, or to remove the lamp, and then commences to show you his goods, your suspicion is aroused, and you conclude that he will try to palm off an inferior article. I more than suspect this to be the little game of the inspiration-depreciators. Whenever a man begins to lower your view of inspiration, it is because he has a trick to play, which is not easily performed in the light. He would hold a *séance* of evil spirits, and therefore he cries, "Let the lights be lowered." We, brethren, are willing to ascribe to the Word of God all the inspiration that can possibly be ascribed to it; and we say boldly that if our preaching is not according to this Word, it is because there is no light in it. We are willing to be tried and tested by it in every way, and we count those to be the noblest of our hearers who search the Scriptures daily to see whether these things be so; but to those who belittle inspiration we will give place by subjection, no, not for an hour.

Do I hear someone say, "But still you must submit to the conclusions of science"? No one is more ready than we are to accept the evident *facts* of science. But what do you mean by science? Is the thing called "science" infallible? Is it not science "falsely so-called"? The history of that human ignorance which calls itself "philosophy" is absolutely identical with the history of fools, except where it diverges into madness. If another Erasmus were to arise and write the history of folly, he would have to give several chapters to philosophy and science, and those chapters would be more telling than any others. I should not myself dare to say that philosophers and scientists are generally fools; but I would give them liberty to speak of one another, and at the close I would say, "Gentlemen, you are less complimentary to each other than I should have been." I would let the wise of each generation speak of the generation that went before it, or nowadays each half of a generation might deal with the previous half generation; for there is little of theory in science today which will survive twenty years, and only a little more which will see the first day of the twentieth century. We travel now at so rapid a rate that we rush by sets of scientific hypotheses as quickly as we pass telegraph posts when riding in an express train. All that we are certain of today is this, that what the learned were sure of a few years ago is now thrown into the limbo of discarded errors. I believe in science, but not in what is called "science." No proven fact in nature is opposed to revelation. The pretty speculations of the pretentious we cannot reconcile with the Bible, and would not if we could. I feel like the man who said, "I can understand in some degree how these great men have found out the weight of the stars, and their distances from one another, and even how, by the spectroscope, they have discovered the materials of which they are composed; but", said he, "I cannot guess how they found out their names." Just so. The fanciful part of science, so dear to many, is what we do not accept. That is the important part of science to many—that part which is a mere guess, for which the guessers fight tooth and nail. The mythology of science is as false as the mythology of the heathen; but this is thing which is made a god of. I say again, as far as its facts are concerned, science is never in conflict with the truths of Holy Scripture, but the hurried deductions drawn from those facts, and the inventions classed as facts, are opposed to Scripture, and necessarily so, because falsehood agrees not with truth.

Two sorts of people have wrought great mischief, and yet they are neither of them worth being considered as judges in the matter: they are both of them disqualified. It is essential than an umpire should know both sides of a question, and neither of these is thus instructed. The first is the irreligious scientist. What does he know about religion? What can he know? He is out of court when the question is—Does science agree with religion? Obviously he who would answer this query must know both of the two things in the question. The second is a better man, but capable of still more mischief. I mean the unscientific Christian, who will trouble his head about reconciling the Bible with science. He had better leave it alone, and not begin his tinkering trade. The mistake made by such men has been that in trying to solve a difficulty, they have either twisted the Bible, or contorted science. The solution has soon been seen to be erroneous, and then we hear the cry that Scripture has been defeated. Not at all; not at all. It is only a vain gloss upon it which has been removed. Here is a good brother who writes a tremendous book, to prove that the six days of creation represent six great geological periods; and he shows how the geological strata, and the organisms thereof, follow very much in the order of the Genesis story of creation. It may be so, or it may be not so; but if anybody should before long show that the strata do not lie in any such order, what would be my reply? I should say that the Bible never taught that they did. The Bible said, "In the beginning God created the heaven and the earth." That leaves any length of time for your fire-ages and your ice-periods, and all that, before the establishment of the present age of man.[1] Then we reach the six days in which the Lord made the heavens and the earth, and rested on the seventh day. There is nothing said about long ages of time, but, on the contrary, "the evening and the morning were the first day", and "the evening and the morning were the second day"; and so on. I do not here lay down any theory, but simply say that if our friend's great book is all fudge, the Bible is not responsible for it. It is true that his theory has an appearance of support from the parallelism which he makes out between the organic life of the ages and that of the seven days; but this may be accounted for from the fact that God usually follows a certain order whether he works in long periods or short ones. I do not know, and I do not care, much about the question; but I want to say that, if you smash up an explanation you must not imagine that you have damaged the Scriptural truth which seemed to require the explanation: you have only burned the wooden palisades with which well-meaning men thought to protect an impregnable fort which needed no such defence. For the most part, we had better leave a difficulty where it is, rather than make another difficulty by our theory. Why make a second hole in the kettle, to mend the first? Especially when the first hole is not there at all, and needs no mending. Believe everything in science which is proved: it will not come to much. You need not fear that your faith will be over-burdened. And then believe everything which is clearly in the Word of God, whether it is proved by outside evidence or not. No proof is needed when God speaks. If he hath said it, this is evidence enough.

But we are told that we ought to give up a part of our old-fashioned theology to save the rest. We are in a carriage travelling over the steppes of Russia. The horses are being driven furiously, but the wolves are close upon us! Can you not see their eyes of fire? The danger is pressing. What must we do? It is proposed that we throw out a child or two. By the time they have eaten the baby, we shall have made a little headway; but should they again overtake us, what then? Why, brave man, *throw out your wife!* 'All that a man hath will he give for his life'; give up nearly every truth in hope of saving one. Throw out inspiration, and let the critics devour it. Throw out election, and all the old Calvinism; here will be a dainty feast for the wolves, and the gentlemen who give us the sage advice will be glad to see the doctrines of grace torn limb from limb. Throw out natural depravity, eternal punishment, and the efficacy of prayer. We have lightened the carriage wonderfully. Now for another drop. *Sacrifice the great sacrifice!* Have done with the atonement!

Brethren, this advice is villainous, and murderous; we will escape these wolves with everything, or we will be lost with everything. It shall be 'the truth, the whole truth, and nothing but the truth', or none at all. We will never attempt to save half the truth by casting any part of it away. The sage advice which has been given us involves treason to God, and disappointment to ourselves. We will stand by all or none. We are told that if we give up something the adversaries will also give up something; but we care not what they will do, for we are not in the least afraid of them. They are not the Imperial conquerors they think themselves. We ask no quarter from their insignificance. We are of the mind of the warrior who was offered presents to buy him off, and he was told that if he accepted so much gold or territory he could return home in triumph, and glory in his easy gain. But he said, 'The Greeks set no store by concessions. They find their glory not in presents, but in spoils.' We shall with the sword of the Spirit maintain the whole truth as ours, and shall not accept a part of it as a grant from the enemies of God. The truth of God we will maintain *as the truth of God*, and we shall not retain it because the philosophic mind consents to our doing so. If scientists agree to our believing a part of the Bible, we thank them for nothing: we believe it whether or no. Their assent is of no more consequence to our faith than the consent of a Frenchman to the Englishman's holding London, or the consent of the mole to the eagle's sight. God being with us we shall not cease from this glorying, but will hold the whole of revealed truth, even to the end.

But now, brethren, while keeping to this first part of my theme, perhaps at too great a length, I say to you that, *believing this, we accept the obligation to preach everything which we see to be in the Word of God, as far as we see it.* We would not wilfully leave out any portion of the whole revelation of God, but we long to be able to say at the last, "We have not shunned to declare unto you the whole counsel of God." What mischief may come of leaving out any portion of the truth, or putting in an alien element! All good men will not agree with me when I say that the addition of infant baptism to the Word of God—for it certainly is not there—is fraught with mischief. Baptismal regeneration rides in upon the shoulders of Pedobaptism. But I speak now of what I know. I have received letters from missionaries, not Baptists, but Wesleyans and Congregationalists, who have said to me, "Since we have been here" (I will not mention the localities lest I get the good men into trouble) "we find a class of persons who are the children of former converts, and who have been baptized, and are therefore called Christians; but they are not one whit better than the heathen around them. They seem to think that they are Christians because of their baptism, and at the same time, being thought Christians by the heathen, their evil lives are perpetual scandal and a dreadful stumbling-block." In many cases this must be so. I only use the fact as an illustration. But suppose it to be either some other error invented, or some great truth neglected, evil will come of it. In the case of the terrible truths known by us as "the terrors of the Lord"; their omission is producing the saddest results. A good man, whom we do not accept as teaching exactly the truth upon this solemn matter, has, nevertheless, most faithfully written again and again to the papers to say that the great weakness of the modern pulpit is that it ignores the justice of God and the punishment of sin. His witness is true, and the evil which he indicates is incalculably great. You cannot leave out that part of the truth which is so dark and so solemn without weakening the force of all the others truths you preach. You rob of their brightness, and their urgent importance, the truths which concern salvation from the wrath to come. Brethren, leave out nothing. Be bold enough to preach unpalatable and unpopular truth. The evil which we may do by adding to, or taking from the Word of the Lord, may not happen in our own days; but if it should come to ripeness in another generation we shall be equally guilty. I have no doubt that the omission of certain truths by the earlier churches led afterwards to serious error; while certain additions in the form of rites and ceremonies, which appeared innocent enough in themselves, led up to Ritualism, and afterwards to the great apostasy of Romanism! Be very careful. Do not go an inch beyond the line of Scripture, and do not stay an inch on this side of it. Keep to the straight line of the Word of God, as far as the Holy Spirit has taught you, and hold back nothing which he has revealed. Be not so bold as to abolish the two ordinances which the Lord Jesus has ordained, though some have ventured upon that gross presumption; neither exaggerate those ordinances into inevitable channels of grace, as others have superstitiously done. Keep you to the revelation of the Spirit. Remember, you will have to give an account, and that account will not be with joy if you have played false with God's truth. Remember the story of Gylippus, to whom Lysander entrusted bags of gold to take to the city authorities. Those bags were tied at the mouth, and then sealed; and Gylippus thought that if he cut the bags at the bottom he might extract a part of the coin, and then he could carefully sew the bottom up again, and so the seals would not be broken, and no one would suspect that gold had been taken. When the bags were opened, to his horror and surprise, there was a note in each bag stating how much it should contain, and so he was detected. The Word of God has self-verifying clauses in it, so that you cannot run away with a part of it, without the remainder of it accusing and convicting you. How will you answer for it "in that day", if you have added to, or taken from the Word of the Lord? I am not here to decide what you ought to consider to be the truth of God; but, whatever you judge it to be, preach it all, and preach it definitely and plainly. If I differ from you, or you from me, we shall not differ very much, if we are equally honest, straightforward, and God-fearing. The way to peace is not concealment of convictions, but the honest expression of them in the power of the Holy Ghost.

One more word. *We accept the obligation to preach all that is in God's Word, definitely and distinctly.* Do not many preach indefinitely, handling the Word of God deceitfully? You might attend upon their ministry for years and not know what they believe. I heard concerning a certain cautious minister, that he was asked by a hearer, "What is your view of the atonement?" He answered, "My dear sir, that is just what I have never told to anybody, and you are not going to get it out of me." This is a strange moral condition for the mind of a preacher of the gospel. I fear that he is not alone in this reticence. They say "they consume their own smoke"; that is to say, they keep their doubts for home consumption. Many dare not say in the pulpit what they say *sub rosâ*,[2] at a private meeting of ministers. Is this honest? I am afraid that it is with some as it was with the schoolmaster in one of the towns of a Southern state in America. A grand old black preacher, one Jasper, had taught his people that the world is as flat as a pancake, and that the sun goes round it every day. This part of his teaching we do not receive; but certain persons had done so, and one of them going to a schoolmaster with his boy, asked, "Do you teach the children that the world is round or flat?" The schoolmaster cautiously answered, "Yes." The enquirer was puzzled, but asked for a clearer answer. "Do you teach your children that the world is round, or that the world is flat?" Then one American dominie answered, *"That* depends upon the opinions of the parents." I suspect that even in Great Britain, in some few cases, a good deal depends upon the leaning of the leading deacon, or the principal subscriber, or the gilded youth in the congregation. If it be so, the crime is loathsome.

But whether for this or for any other cause we teach with double tongue, the result will be highly injurious. I venture here to quote a story which I heard from a beloved brother. A cadger called upon a minister to extract money from him. The good man did not like the beggar's appearance much, and he said to him, "I do not care for your case, and I see no special reason why you should come to me." The beggar replied, "I am sure you would help me if you knew what great benefit I have received from your blessed ministry." "What is that?" said the pastor. The beggar then replied, "Why, sir, when I first came to hear you I cared neither for God nor devil, but now, under your blessed ministry, *I have come to love them both.*" What marvel if, under some men's shifty talk, people grow into love of both truth and falsehood! People will say, "We like this form of doctrine, and we like the other also." The fact is, they would like anything if only a clever deceiver would put it plausibly before them. They admire Moses and Aaron, but they would not say a word against Jannes and Jambres. We shall not join in the confederacy which seems to aim at such a comprehension. We must preach the gospel so distinctly that our people know what we are preaching. "If the trumpet give an uncertain sound, who shall prepare himself for the battle?" Don't puzzle your people with doubtful speeches. "Well", said one, "I had a new idea the other day. I did not enlarge upon it; but I just threw it out." That is a very good thing to do with most of your new ideas. Throw them out, by all means; but mind where you are when you do it; for if you throw them out from the pulpit they may strike somebody, and inflict a wound upon faith. Throw out your fancies, but first go alone in a boat a mile out to sea. When you have once thrown out your unconsidered trifles, leave them to the fishes.

We have nowadays around us a class of men who preach Christ, and even preach the gospel; but then they preach a great deal else which is not true, and thus they destroy the good of all that they deliver, and lure men to error. They would be styled "evangelical" and yet be of the school which is really anti-evangelical. Look well to these gentlemen. I have heard that a fox, when close hunted by the dogs, will pretend to be one of them, and run with the pack. That is what certain are aiming at just now: *the foxes would seem to be dogs.* But in the case of the fox, his strong scent betrays him, and the dogs soon find him out; and even so, the scent of false doctrine is not easily concealed, and the game does not answer for long. There are extant ministers of whom we scarce can tell whether they are dogs or foxes; but all men shall know our quality as long as we live, and they shall be in no doubt as to what we believe and teach. We shall not hesitate to speak in the strongest Saxon words we can find, and in the plainest sentences we can put together, that which we hold as fundamental truth.

Thus I have been all this while upon my first head, and the other two must, therefore, occupy less time, though I judge them to be of the first importance.

Our Army

NOW we must review OUR ARMY.

What can individual men do in a great crusade? We are associated with all the people of the Lord. We need for comrades the members of our churches; these must go out and win souls for Christ. We need the co-operation of the entire brotherhood and sisterhood. What is to be accomplished unless the saved ones go forth, all of them, for the salvation of others? But the question now is mooted, *Is there to be a church at all?* Is there to be a distinct army of saints, or are we to include atheists? You have heard of "the church of the future" which we are to have in*stead* [3] of the church of Jesus Christ. As its extreme lines will take in atheists, we may hope, in our charity, that it will include evil spirits also. What a wonderful church it will be, certainly, when we see it! It will be anything else you like, but not a church. When the soldiers of Christ shall have included in their ranks all the banditti of the adversary, will there be any army for Christ at all? Is it not distinctly a capitulation at the very beginning of the war? So I take it to be.

We must not only believe in the church of God, but recognize it very distinctly. Some denominations recognize anything and everything more than the church. Such a thing as a meeting of the church is unknown. In some "the church" signifies the ministers or clergy; but in truth it should signify the whole body of the faithful, and there should be an opportunity for these to meet together to act as a church. It is, I judge, for the church of God to carry on the work of God in the land. The final power and direction is with our Lord Jesus, and under him it should lie, not with some few who are chosen by delegation or by patronage, but with the whole body of believers. We must more and more acknowledge the church which

God has committed to our charge; and in so doing, we shall evoke a strength which else lies dormant. If the church is recognized by Christ Jesus, it is worthy to be recognized by us; for we are the servants of the church.

Yes, we believe that there ought to be a church. But churches are very disappointing things. Every pastor of a large church will own this in his own soul. I do not know that the churches of today are any worse than they used to be in Paul's time, or any better. The churches at Corinth and Laodicea and other cities exhibited grave faults; and if there are faults in ours, let us not be amazed; but yet let us grieve over such things, and labour after a higher standard. Albeit that the members of our church are not all they ought to be, neither are we ourselves. Yet, if I went anywhere for choice company, I should certainly resort to the members of my church.

> "These are the company I keep:
> These are the choicest friends I know."

O Jerusalem, with all thy faults, I love thee still! The people of God are still the aristocracy of the race: God bless them! Yes, we mean to have a church.

Now, *is that church to be real or statistical?* That depends very much upon you, dear brethren. I would urge upon you the resolve to have no church unless it be a real one. The fact is, that too frequently religious statistics are shockingly false. Cooking of such accounts is not an unknown art in certain quarters, as we know. I heard of one case the other day where an increase of four was reported; but had the roll been amended in the least, there must have been a decrease of twenty-five. Is it not falsehood when numbers are manipulated? There is a way of making figures figure as they should not figure. Never do this. Let us not keep names on our books when they are only names. Certain of the good old people like to keep them there, and cannot bear to have them removed; but when you do not know where individuals are, nor what they are, how can you count them? They are gone to America, or Australia, or to heaven, but as far as your roll is concerned they are with you still. Is this a right thing? It may not be possible to be absolutely accurate, but let us aim at it. We ought to look upon this in a very serious light, and purge ourselves of the vice of false reporting; for God himself will not bless mere names. It is not his way to work with those who play a false part. If there is not a real person for each name, amend your list. Keep your church real and effective, or make no report. A merely nominal church is a lie. Let it be what it professes to be. We may not glory in statistics; but we ought to know the facts.

But is this church to increase, or is it to die out? It will do either the one or the other. We shall see our friends going to heaven, and, if there are no young men and young women converted and brought in and added to us, the church on earth will have emigrated to the church triumphant above; and what is to be done for the cause and the kingdom of the Master here below? We should be crying, praying, and pleading that the church may continually grow. We must preach, visit, pray, and labour for this end. May the Lord add unto us daily such as are saved! If there be no harvest, can the seed be the true seed? Are we preaching apostolic doctrine if we never see apostolic results? Oh, my brethren, our hearts should be ready to break if there be no increase in the flocks we tend. O Lord, we beseech thee, send now prosperity!

If a church is to be what it ought to be for the purposes of God, *we must train it in the holy art of prayer.* Churches without prayer-meetings are grievously common. Even if there were only one such, it would be one to weep over. In many churches the prayer-meeting is only the skeleton of a gathering: the form is kept up, but the people do not come. There is no interest, no power, in connection with the meeting. Oh, my brothers, let it not be so with you! Do train the people to continually meet together for prayer. Rouse them to incessant supplication. There is a holy art in it. Study to show yourselves approved by the prayerfulness of your people. If you pray yourself, you will want them to pray with you; and when they begin to pray with you, and for you, and for the work of the Lord, they will want more prayer themselves, and the appetite will grow. Believe me, if a church does not pray, it is dead. Instead of putting united prayer last, put it first. Everything will hinge upon the power of prayer in the church.

We ought to have our churches all busy for God. What is the use of a church that simply assembles to hear sermons, even as a family gathers to eat its meals? What, I say, if the profit, if it does no work? Are not many professors sadly indolent in the Lord's work, though diligent enough in their own? Because of Christian idleness we hear of the necessity for amusements, and all sorts of nonsense. If they were at work for the Lord Jesus we should not hear of this. A good woman said to a housewife, "Mrs. So-and-so, how do you manage to amuse yourself?" "Why", she replied, "my dear, you see there are so many children that there is much work to be done in my house." "Yes", said the other, "I see it. I see that there is much work to be done in your house; but as it never is done, I was wondering how you amused yourself." Much needs to be done by a Christian church within its own bounds, and for the neighbourhood, and for the poor and the fallen, and for the heathen world, and so forth; and if it is well attended to, minds, and hearts, and hands, and tongues will be occupied, and diversions will not be asked for. Let idleness come in, and that spirit which rules lazy people, and there will arise a desire to be amused. What amusements they are, too! If religion is not a farce with some congregations, at any rate they turn out better to see a farce than to unite in prayer. I cannot understand it. The man who is all aglow with love to Jesus finds little need for amusement. He has no time for trifling. He is in dead earnest to save souls, and establish the truth, and enlarge the kingdom of his Lord. There has always been some pressing claim for the cause of God upon me; and, that settled, there has been another, and another, and another, and the scramble has been to find opportunity to do the work that must be done, and hence I have not had the time for gadding abroad after frivolities. Oh, to get a working church! The German churches, when our dear friend, Mr. Oncken, was alive, always carried out the rule of asking every member, "What are you going to do for Christ?" and they put the answer down in a book. The one thing that was required of every member was that he should continue doing something for the Saviour. If he ceased to do anything it was a matter for church discipline, for he was an idle professor, and could not be allowed to remain in the church like a drone in a hive of working bees. He must do or go. Oh, for a vineyard without a barren fig-tree to cumber the ground! At present the most of our sacred warfare is carried on by a small body of intensely living, earnest people, and the rest are either in hospital, or are mere camp followers. We are thankful for that consecrated few; but we pine to see the altar fire consuming all that is professedly laid upon the altar.

Brethren, *we want churches also that produce saints;* men of mighty faith and prevalent prayer; men of holy living, and of consecrated giving; men filled with the Holy Spirit. We must have these saints as rich clusters, or surely we are not branches of the true vine. I would desire to see in every church a Mary sitting at Jesus' feet, a Martha serving Jesus, a Peter and a John; but the best name for a church is "All Saints." All believers should be saints, and all may be saints. We have no connection with "the latter-day saints", but we love everyday saints. Oh, for more of them! If God shall so help us that the whole company of the faithful shall, each one of them individually, come to the fulness of the stature of a man in Christ Jesus, then we shall see greater things than these. Glorious times will come when believers have glorious characters.

We want also churches that know the truth, and are well taught in the things of God. What do some Christian people know? They come and hear, and, in the plenitude of your wisdom, you instruct them; but how little they receive to lay by in store for edification! Brethren, the fault lies partly with us, and partly with themselves. If we taught better they would learn better. See how little many professors know; not enough to give them discernment between living truth and deadly error. Old-fashioned believers could give you chapter and verse for what they believed; but how few of such remain! Our venerable grandsires were at home when conversing upon "the covenants." I love men who love the covenant of grace, and base their divinity upon it: the doctrine of the covenants is the key of theology. They that feared the Lord spake often one to another. They used to speak of everlasting life, and all that comes of it. They had a good argument for this belief, and an excellent reason for that other doctrine; and to try to shake them was by no means a hopeful task: you might as well have hoped to shake the pillars of the universe; for they were steadfast, and could not be carried about with every wind of doctrine. They knew what they knew, and they held fast that which they had learned. What is to become of our country, with the present deluge of Romanism pouring upon us through the ritualistic party, unless our churches abound in firm believers who can discern between the regeneration of the Holy Spirit and its ceremonial substitute? What is to become of our churches in this day of skepticism, when every fixed truth is pointed at with the finger of doubt, unless our people have the truths of the gospel written in their hearts? Oh, for a church of out-and-out believers, impervious to the soul-destroying doubt which pours upon us in showers!

Yet all this would not reach our ideal. *We want a church of a missionary character,* which will go forth to gather out a people unto God from all parts of the world. A church is a soul-saving company, or it is nothing. If the salt exercises no preserving influence on that which surrounds it, what is the use of it? Yet some shrink from effort in their immediate neighbourhood because of the poverty and vice of the people. I remember a minister who is now deceased, a very good man he was, too, in many respects; but he utterly amazed me by a reply which he made to a question of mine. I remarked that he had an awful neighbourhood round his chapel, and, I said, "Are you able to do much for them?" He answered, "No, I feel almost glad that we keep clear of them; for, you see, if any of them were converted, it would be a fearful burden upon us." I knew him to be the soul of caution and prudence, but this took me aback, and I sought an explanation. "Well," he said, "we should have to keep them: they are mostly thieves and harlots, and if converted they would have no means of livelihood, and we are a poor people, and could not support them"! He was a devout man, and one with whom it was to one's profit to converse; and yet that was how he had gradually come to look at the case. His people with difficulty sustained the expenses of worship, and thus chill penury repressed a gracious zeal, and froze the genial current of his soul. There was a great deal of common sense in what he said, but yet it was an awful thing to be able to say it. We want a people who will not for ever sing,—

> "We are a garden walled around,
> Chosen and made peculiar ground;
> A little spot enclosed by grace,
> Out of the world's wild wilderness."

It is good verse for occasional singing, but not when it comes to mean, "We are very few, and we wish to be." No, no, brethren! we are a little detachment of the King's soldiers detained in a foreign country upon garrison duty; yet we mean not only to hold the fort, but to add territory to our Lord's dominion. We are not to be driven out; but, on the contrary, we are going to drive out the Canaanites; for this land belongs to us, it is given to us of the Lord, and we will subdue it. May we be fired with the spirit of discoverers and conquerors, and never rest while there yet remains a class to be rescued, a region to be evangelized!

We are rowing like lifeboat men upon a stormy sea, and we are hurrying to yonder wreck, where men are perishing. If we may not draw that old wreck to shore, we will at least, by the power of God, rescue the perishing, save life, and bear the redeemed to the shores of salvation. Our mission, like our Lord's, is to gather out the chosen of God from among men, that they may live to the glory of God. Every saved man should be, under God, a saviour; and the church is not in a right state until she has reached that conception of herself. The elect church is saved that she may save, cleansed that she may cleanse, blessed that she may bless. All the world is the field, and all the members of the church should work therein for the great Husbandman. Waste lands are to be reclaimed, and forests broken up by the plough, till the solitary place begins to blossom as the rose. We must not be content with holding our own: we must invade the territories of the prince of darkness.

My brethren, what is our relation to this church? What is our position in it? *We are servants.* May we always know our place, and keep it! The highest place in the church will always come to the man who willingly chooses the lowest; while he that aspires to be great among his brethren will sink to be least of all. Certain men might have been something if they had not thought themselves so. A consciously great man is an evidently little one. A lord over God's heritage is a base usurper. He that in his heart and soul is always ready to serve the very least of the family; who expects to be put upon; and willingly sacrifices reputation and friendship for Christ's sake, he shall fulfil a heaven-sent ministry. We are not sent to be ministered unto, but to minister. Let us sing unto our Well-Beloved:—

> "There's not a lamb in all thy flock,
> I would disdain to feed;
> There's not a foe before whose face
> I'd fear thy cause to plead."

We must also be examples to the flock. He that cannot be safely imitated ought not to be tolerated in a pulpit. Did I hear of a minister who was always disputing for pre-eminence? Or of another who was mean and covetous? Or of a third whose conversation was not always chaste? Or of a fourth who did not rise, as a rule, till eleven o'clock in the morning? I would hope that this last rumour was altogether false. An idle minister—what will become of him? A pastor who neglects his office? Does he expect to go to heaven? I was about to say, "If he does go there at all, may it be soon." A lazy minister is a creature despised of men, and abhorred of God. "You give your minister only £50 a year!" I said, to a farmer. "Why, the poor man cannot live on it." The answer was, "Look here, sir! I tell you what: we give him a good deal more than he earns." It is a sad pity when that can be said; it is an injury to all those who follow our sacred calling. We are to be examples to our flock in all things. In all diligence, in all gentleness, in all humility, and in all holiness we are to excel. When Caesar went on his wars, one thing always helped his soldiers to bear hardships: they knew that Caesar fared as they fared. He marched if they marched, he thirsted if they thirsted, and he was always in the heart of the battle if they were fighting. We must do more than others if we are officers in Christ's army. We must not cry, "Go on", but, "Come on." Our people may justly expect of us, at the very least, that we should be among the most self-denying, the most laborious, and the most earnest in the church, *and somewhat more.* We cannot expect to see holy churches if we who are bound to be their examples are unsanctified. If there be, in any of our brethren, consecration and sanctification, evident to all men, God has blessed them, and God will bless them more and more. If these be lacking in us, we need not search far to find the cause of our non-success.

I have many things to say to you, but you cannot bear them now, because the time is long and you are weary. I desire, however, if you can gather up your patience and your strength, to dwell for a little upon the most important part of my triple theme. Here suffer me to pray for his help, whose name and person I would magnify. Come, Holy Spirit, heavenly Dove, and rest upon us now!

Our Strength

GRANTED that we preach the Word alone; granted that we are surrounded by a model church, which, alas, is not always the case; but, granted that it is so, OUR STRENGTH is the next consideration. This must come from THE SPIRIT OF GOD. We believe in the Holy Ghost, and in our absolute dependence upon him. We believe; but do we believe *practically?* Brethren, as to ourselves and our own work, do we believe in the Holy Ghost? Do we believe because we habitually prove the truth of the doctrine?

We must depend upon the Spirit in our preparations. Is this the fact with us all? Are you in the habit of working your way into the meaning of texts by the guidance of the Holy Spirit? Every man that goes to the land of heavenly knowledge must work his passage thither; but he must work out his passage in the strength of the Holy Spirit, or he will arrive at some island in the sea of fancy, and never set his foot upon the sacred shores of the truth. You do not know the truth, my brother, because you have read "Hodge's Outlines", or "Fuller's Gospel worthy of all Acceptation"; or "Owen on the Spirit", or any other classic of our faith. You do not know the truth, my brother, merely because you accept the Westminster Assembly's Confession, and have studied it perfectly. No, we know nothing till we are taught of the Holy Ghost, who speaks to the heart rather than to the ear. It is a wonderful fact that we do not even hear the voice of Jesus till the Spirit rests upon us. John says, "I was in the Spirit on the Lord's day, and I heard a voice behind me." He heard not that voice till he was in the Spirit. How many heavenly words we miss because we abide not in the Spirit!

We cannot succeed in supplication except the Holy Ghost helpeth our infirmities, for true prayer is "praying in the Holy Ghost." The Spirit makes an atmosphere around every living prayer, and within that circle prayer lives and prevails; outside of it prayer is a dead formality. As to ourselves, then, in our study, in prayer, in thought, in word, and in deed, we must depend upon the Holy Ghost.

In the pulpit do we really and truly rest upon the aid of the Spirit. I do not censure any brother for his mode of preaching, but I must confess that it seems very odd to me when a brother prays that the

111

Holy Ghost may help him in preaching, and then I see him put his hand behind him and draw a manuscript out of his pocket, so fashioned that he can place it in the middle of his Bible, and read from it without being suspected of doing so. These precautions for ensuring secrecy look as though the man was a little ashamed of his paper; but I think he should be far more ashamed of his precautions. Does he expect the Spirit of God to bless him while he is practising a trick? And how can He help him when he reads out of a paper from which anyone else might read without the Spirit's aid? What has the Holy Ghost to do with the business? Truly, he may have had something to do with the manuscript in the composing of it, but in the pulpit his aid is superfluous. The truer thing would be to thank the Holy Spirit for assistance rendered, and ask that what he has enabled us to get into our pockets may now enter the people's hearts. Still, if the Holy Ghost should have anything to say to the people that is not in the paper, how can he say it by us? He seems to me to be very effectually blocked as to freshness of utterance by that method of ministry. Still, it is not for me to censure, although I may quietly plead for liberty in prophesying, and room for the Lord to give us in the same hour what we shall speak.

Furthermore, we must depend upon the Spirit of God as to our results. No man among us really thinks that he could regenerate a soul. We are not so foolish as to claim power to change a heart of stone. We may not dare to presume quite so far as this, and yet we may come to think that, by our experience, we can help people over spiritual difficulties. Can we? We may be hopeful that our enthusiasm will drive the living church before us, and drag the dead world after us. Will it be so? Perhaps we imagine that if we could only *get up* a revival, we should easily secure large additions to the church? Is it worth while to *get up* a revival? Are not all true revivals to be *got down*? We may persuade ourselves that drums and trumpets and shouting will do a great deal. But, my brethren, "the Lord is not in the wind." Results worth having come from that silent but omnipotent Worker whose name is the Spirit of God: in him, and in him only, must we trust for the conversion of a single Sunday-school child, and for every genuine revival. For the keeping of our people together, and for the building of them up into a holy temple, we must look to him. The Spirit might say, even as our Lord did, "Without me ye can do nothing."

What is the Church of God without the Holy Ghost? Ask what would Hermon be without its dew, or Egypt without its Nile? Behold the land of Canaan when the curse of Elias fell upon it, and for three years it felt neither dew nor rain: such would Christendom become without the Spirit. What the valleys would be without their brooks, or the cities without their wells; what the corn-fields would be without the sun, or the vintage without the summer—that would our churches be without the Spirit. As well think of day without light, or life without breath, or heaven without God, as of Christian service without the Holy Spirit. Nothing can supply his place if he be absent: the pastures are a desert, the fruitful fields are a wilderness, Sharon languishes, and Carmel is burned with fire. Blessed Spirit of the Lord, forgive us that we have done thee such despite, by our forgetfulness of thee, by our proud self-sufficiency, by resisting thine influences, and quenching thy fire! Henceforth work in us according to thine own excellence. Make our hearts tenderly impressible, and then turn us as wax to the seal, and stamp upon us the image of the Son of God. With some such prayer and confession of faith as this, let us pursue our subject in the power of the good Spirit of whom we speak.

What does the Holy Ghost do? Beloved, what is there of good work that he does not do? It is his to quicken, to convince, to illuminate, to cleanse, to guide, to preserve, to console, to confirm, to perfect, and to use. How much might be said under each one of these heads! It is he that worketh in us to will and to do. He that hath wrought all things is God. Glory be unto the Holy Ghost for all that he has accomplished in such poor, imperfect natures as ours! We can do nothing apart from the life-sap which flows to us from Jesus the Vine. That which is our own is fit only to cause us shame and confusion of face. We never go a step towards heaven without the Holy Ghost. We never lead another on the heavenward road without the Holy Ghost. We have no acceptable thought, or word, or deed, apart from the Holy Spirit. Even the uplifting of the eye and hope, or the ejaculatory prayer of the heart's desire, must be his work. All good things are of him and through him, from beginning to end. There is no fear of exaggerating here. Do we, however, translate this conviction into our actual procedure?

Instead of dilating upon what the Spirit of God does, let me refer to your experience, and ask you a question or two. Do you remember times when the Spirit of God has been graciously present in fulness of power with you and with your people? What seasons those have been! That Sabbath was a high day. Those services were like the worship of Jacob when he said, "Surely God was in this place!" What mutual telegraphing goes on between the preacher in the Spirit and the people in the Spirit! Their eyes seem to talk to us as much as our tongues talk to them. They are then a very different people from what they are on common occasions: there is even a beauty upon their faces while we are glorifying the Lord Jesus, and they are enjoying and drinking in our testimony. Have you ever seen a gentleman of the modern school enjoying his own preaching? Our evangelical preachers are very happy in delivering what our liberal friends are pleased to call their "platitudes"; but the moderns in their wisdom feel no such joy. Can you imagine a Downgrader in the glow which our Welsh friends call the *"Hwyl"*? How grimly they descant upon the *Post Exilic theory!* They remind me of Ruskin's expression—"Turner had no joy of his mill." I grant you, there is nothing to enjoy, and they are evidently glad to get through their task of piling up meatless bones. They stand at an empty manger, amusing themselves by biting their crib. They get through their preaching, and they are dull enough till Monday comes with a football match, or an entertainment in the school-room, or a political meeting. To them preaching is "work", though they don't put much work into it. The old preachers, and some of those who now live, but are said to be "obsolete", think the pulpit a throne, or a triumphal chariot, and are near heaven when helped to preach with power. Poor fools that we are, preaching our "antiquated" gospel! We do enjoy the task. Our gloomy doctrines make us very happy. Strange, is it not? The gospel is evidently marrow and fatness to us, and our beliefs—albeit, of course, they are very absurd and unphilosophical—do content us, and make us very confident and happy. I may say of some of my brethren, that their very eyes seem to sparkle, and their souls to glow, while enlarging upon free grace and dying love. It is so, brethren, that when we have the presence of God, then we and our hearers are carried away with heavenly delight. Nor is this all. When the Spirit of God is present every saint loves his fellow saint, and there is no strife among us unless it be who shall be the most loving. Then prayer is wrestling and prevailing, and ministry is sowing good seed and reaping large sheaves. Then conversions are plentiful, restorations are abundant, and advances in grace are seen on every side. Hallelujah! With the Spirit of God all goes well.

But do you know the opposite condition? I hope you do not. It is death in life. I trust you have never, in your scientific experiments, been cruel enough to put a mouse under an air pump, and gradually to exhaust the receiver. I have read of the fatal experiment. Alas, poor mouse! As the air gets thinner and thinner, how great his sufferings, and when it is all gone, there he lies—dead. Have you never yourself been under an exhausted receiver, spiritually? You have only been there long enough to perceive that the sooner you escaped, the better for you. Said one to me the other day, "Well, as to the sermon which I heard from the modern-thought divine, there was no great harm in it; for on this occasion he kept clear of false doctrine; but the whole affair was so intensely cold. I felt like a man who has fallen down a crevasse in a glacier: and I felt shut up as if I could not breathe the air of heaven." You know that arctic cold; and it may occasionally be felt even where the doctrine is sound. When the Spirit of God is gone, even truth itself becomes an iceberg. How wretched is religion frozen and lifeless! The Holy Ghost has gone, and all energy and enthusiasm have gone with him. The scene becomes like that described in the Ancient Mariner, when the ship was becalmed:—

> "The very deep did rot,
> Alas, that ever this should be!
> Yea, slimy things did crawl with legs
> Upon the slimy sea."

Within the ship all was death. And we have seen it so within a church. I am tempted to apply Coleridge's lines to much that is to be seen in those churches which deserve the name of "congregations of the dead." He describes how the bodies of the dead were inspired and the ship moved on, each dead man fulfilling his office in a dead and formal fashion:—

> "The helmsman steered, the ship moved on;
> Yet never a breeze up blew;
> The mariners all 'gan work the ropes,

> Where they were wont to do;
> They raised their limbs like lifeless tools—
> We were a ghastly crew."

All living fellowship was lacking, for the Ancient Mariner says:—

> "The body of my brother's son
> Stood by me, knee to knee:
> The body and I pulled at one rope,
> But he said nought to me."

It is much the same in those "respectable" congregations where no man knows his fellow, and a dignified isolation supplants all saintly communion. To the preacher, if he be the only living man in the company, the church affords very dreary society. His sermons fall on ears that hear them not aright.

> "Twas night, calm night, the moon was high;
> The dead men stood together.
> All stood together on the deck
> For a charnel-dungeon fitter:
> All fixed on me their stony eyes,
> That in the moon did glitter."

Yes, the preacher's moonlight, cold and cheerless, falls on faces which are like it. The discourse impresses their stolid intellects, and fixes their stony eyes; but hearts! Well, hearts are not in fashion in those regions. Hearts are for the realm of life; but without the Holy Spirit what do congregations know of true life? If the Holy Ghost has gone, death reigns, and the church is a sepulchre. Therefore we must entreat him to abide with us, and we must never rest till he does so. O brothers, let it not be that I talk to you about this, and that then we permit the matter to drop; but let us each one with heart and soul seek to have the power of the Holy Spirit abiding upon him.

Have we received the Holy Ghost? Is he with us now? If so it be, *how can we secure his future presence?* How can we constrain him to abide with us?

I would say, first, *treat him as he should be treated.* Worship him as the adorable Lord God. Never call the Holy Spirit "it"; nor speak of him as if he were a doctrine, or an influence, or an orthodox myth. Reverence him, love him, and trust him with familiar yet reverent confidence. He is God, let him be God to you.

See to it that you act in conformity with his working. The mariner to the East cannot create the winds at his pleasure, but he knows when the trade winds blow, and he takes advantage of the season to speed his vessel. Put out to sea in holy enterprise when the heavenly wind is with you. Take the sacred tide at its flood. Increase your meetings when you feel that the Spirit of God is blessing them. Press home the truth more earnestly than ever when the Lord is opening ears and hearts to accept it. You will soon know when there is dew about, prize the gracious visitation. The farmer says, "Make hay while the sun shines." You cannot make the sun shine; that is quite out of your power; but you can use the sun while he shines. "When thou hearest the sound of a going in the tops of the mulberry trees, then thou shalt bestir thyself." Be diligent in season and out of season; but in a lively season be doubly laborious.

Evermore, in beginning, in continuing, and in ending any and every good work, *consciously and in very truth depend upon the Holy Ghost.* Even a sense of your need of him he must give you; and the prayers with which you entreat him to come must come from him. You are engaged in a work so spiritual, so far above all human power, that to forget the Spirit is to ensure defeat. Make the Holy Ghost to be the *sine quâ non* of your efforts, and go so far as to say to him, "If thy presence go not with us, carry us not up hence." Rest only in him and then *reserve for him all the glory.* Be specially mindful of this, for this is a tender point with him: he will not give his glory to another. Take care to praise the Spirit of God from your inmost heart, and gratefully wonder that he should condescend to work by you. Please him by glorifying Christ. Render him homage by yielding yourself to his impulses, and by hating everything that grieves him. The consecration of your whole being will be the best psalm in his praise.

There are a few things which I would have you remember, and then I have done. Remember that the Holy Spirit has his ways and methods, and there are some things which he will not do. Bethink you that *he makes no promise to bless compromises.* If we make a treaty with error or sin, we do it at our own risk. If we do anything that we are not clear about, if we tamper with truth or holiness, if we are friends of the world, if we make provision for the flesh, if we preach half-heartedly and are in league with errorists, we have no promise that the Holy Spirit will go with us. The great promise runs in quite another strain: "Come ye out from among them, and be ye separate, saith the Lord, and touch not the unclean thing; and I will receive you, and will be a Father unto you, and ye shall be my sons and daughters, saith the Lord God Almighty." In the New Testament only in that one place, with the exception of the Book of Revelation, is God called by the name of "the Lord God Almighty." If you want to know what great things the Lord can do, as the Lord God Almighty, be separate from the world, and from those who apostatize from the truth. The title, "Lord God Almighty" is evidently quoted from the Old Testament. "El-Shaddai", God all-sufficient, the many-breasted God. We shall never know the utmost power of God for supplying all our needs till we have cut connection once for all with everything which is not according to His mind. That was grand of Abraham when he said to the king of Sodom, "I will not take of thee,"—a Babylonish garment, or a wedge of gold? No, no. He said, "I will not take from a thread even to a shoe latchet." That was "the cut direct." The man of God will have nothing to do with Sodom, or with false doctrine. If you see anything that is evil, give it the cut direct. Have done with those who have done with truth. Then you will be prepared to receive the promise, and not till then.

Dear brethren, remember that wherever there is great love, there is sure to be great jealousy. "Love is strong as death." What next? "Jealousy is cruel as the grave." "God is love"; and for that very reason "The Lord thy God is a jealous God." Keep clear of everything that defiles, or that would grieve the Holy Spirit; for if he be vexed with us, we shall soon be put to shame before the enemy.

Note, next, that *he makes no promise to cowardice*. If you allow the fear of man to rule you, and wish to save self from suffering or ridicule, you will find small comfort in the promise of God. "He that saveth his life shall lose it." The promises of the Holy Spirit to us in our warfare are to those who quit themselves like men, and by faith are made brave in the hour of conflict. I wish that we were come to this pass, that we utterly despised ridicule and calumny. Oh, to have the self-oblivion of that Italian martyr of whom Foxe speaks! They condemned him to be burned alive, and he heard the sentence calmly. But, you know, burning martyrs, however delightful, is also expensive; and the mayor of the town did not care to pay for the fagots, and the priests who had accused him also wished to do the work without personal expense. So they had an angry squabble, and there stood the poor man for whose benefits these fagots were to be contributed, quietly hearing their mutual recriminations. Finding that they could not settle it, he said: "Gentlemen, I will end your dispute. It is a pity that you should, either of you, be at so much expense to find fagots for my burning, and, for my Lord's sake, I will even pay for the wood that burns me, if you please." There is a fine touch of scorn as well as meekness there. I do not know that I would have paid that bill; but I have even felt inclined to go a little out of the way to help the enemies of the truth to find fuel for their criticisms of me. Yes, yes; I will yet be more vile, and give them more to complain of. I will go through with the controversy for Christ's sake, and do nothing whatever to quiet their wrath. Brethren, if you trim a little, if you try to save a little of your repute with the men of the apostasy, it will go ill with you. He that is ashamed of Christ and his Word in this evil generation shall find that Christ is ashamed of him at the last.

I will be very brief on these points. Remember, next, that *the Holy Ghost will never set his seal to falsehood.* Never! If what you preach is not the truth, God will not own it. See ye well to this.

What is more, *the Holy Ghost never sets his signature to a blank.* That would be unwise on the part of man, and the holy Lord will not perpetrate such a folly. If we do not speak clear doctrine with plainness of speech, the Holy Ghost will not put his signature to our empty prating. If we do not come out distinctly with Christ and him crucified, we may say farewell to true success.

Next, remember that *the Holy Ghost will never sanction sin;* and to bless the ministry of some men would be to sanction their evil ways. "Be ye clean, that bear the vessels of the Lord." Let your character correspond with your teaching, and let your churches be purged from open transgressors, lest the Holy Ghost disown your teaching, not for its own sake, but because of the ill savour of unholy living which dishonours it.

Remember, again, that *he will never encourage idleness.* The Holy Ghost will not come to rescue us from the consequences of wilful neglect of the Word of God and study. If we allow ourselves to go up and down all the week doing nothing, we may not climb the pulpit stairs and dream that the Lord will be there and then tell us what to speak. If help were promised to such, then the lazier the man the better the sermon. If the Holy Spirit worked only by impromptu speakers, the less we read our Bibles and the less we meditated on them the better. If it be wrong to quote from books, "attention to reading" should not have been commanded. All this is obviously absurd, and not one of you will fall into such a delusion. We are bound to be much in meditation, and give ourselves wholly to the Word of God and prayer, and when we have minded these things we may look for the Spirit's approbation and co-operation. We ought to prepare the sermon as if all depended upon us, and then we are to trust the Spirit of God knowing that all depends upon Him. The Holy Ghost sends no one into the harvest to sleep among the sheaves, but to bear the burden and heat of the day. We may well pray God to send more *"labourers"* into the vineyard; for the Spirit will be with the strength of labourers, but he will not be the friend of loiterers.

Recollect, again, that *the Holy Ghost will not bless us in order to sustain our pride.* Is it not possible that we may be wishing for a great blessing that we may be thought great men? This will hinder our success: the string of the bow is out of order and the arrow will turn aside. What does God do with men that are proud? Does he exalt them? I trow not. Herod made an eloquent oration, and he put on a dazzling silver robe which glistened in the sun, and when the people saw his vestments and listened to his charming voice, they cried, "It is the voice of a god, and not of a man"; but the Lord smote him, and he was eaten of worms. Worms have a prescriptive right to proud flesh; and when we get very mighty and very big, the worms expect to make a meal of us. "Pride goeth before destruction, and a haughty spirit before a fall." Keep humble if you would have the Spirit of God with you. The Holy Ghost takes no pleasure in the inflated oratory of the proud; how can he? Would you have him sanction bombast? "Walk humbly with thy God", O preacher! for thou canst not walk with him in any other fashion; and if thou walk not with him, thy walking will be vain.

Consider, again, that *the Holy Ghost will not dwell where there is strife.* Let us follow peace with all men, and specially let us keep peace in our churches. Some of you are not yet favoured with this boon; and possibly it is not your fault. You have inherited old feuds. In many a small community, all the members of the congregation are cousins to one another, and relations usually agree to disagree. When cousins cozen their cousins, the seeds of illwill are sown, and these intrude even into church life. Your predecessor's high-handedness in past time may breed a good deal of quarrelling for many years to come. He was a man of war from his youth, and even when he is gone the spirits which he called from the vasty deep remain to haunt the spot. I fear you cannot expect much blessing, for the Holy Dove does not dwell by troubled waters: he chooses to come where brotherly love continues. For great principles, and matters of holy discipline, we may risk peace itself; but for self or party may such conduct be far from us.

Lastly, remember *the Holy Ghost will only bless in conformity with His own set purpose.* Our Lord explains what that purpose is: "He shall glorify me." He has come forth for this grand end, and he will not put up with anything short of it. If, then, we do not preach Christ, what is the Holy Ghost to do with our preaching? If we do not make the Lord Jesus glorious; if we do not lift him high in the esteem of men, if we do not labour to make him King of kings, and Lord of lords; we shall not have the Holy Spirit with us. Vain will be rhetoric, music, architecture, energy, and social status: if our one design be not to magnify the Lord Jesus, we shall work alone and work in vain.

This is all I have to say to you at this time; but, my dear brethren, it is a great all if first considered, and then carried out. May it have practical effect upon us! It will, if the great Worker uses it, and not else. Go forth, O soldiers of Jesus, with "the sword of the Spirit, which is the word of God." Go forth with the companies of the godly whom you lead, and let every man be strong in the Lord, and in the power of his might. As men alive from the dead, go forth in the quickening power of the Holy Ghost: you have no other strength. May the blessing of the Triune God rest upon you, one and all, for the Lord Jesus Christ's sake! Amen.

Notes

1. Spurgeon held to a version of "the gap theory"—the notion that fire-and ice-ages fit into a gap between Genesis 1:1 and 1:2. Few evangelical scholars today hold to that view, but it was quite popular in Spurgeon's day.
2. Privately.
3. At this point, the audience could not be restrained, but stopped the speaker with cheers and laughter, to which he answered, "Nay, do not stop me in the middle of a sentence. My rule is not to mention names, and yet you have found a name hidden in a harmless word."

A PURITAN CATECHISM

With Proofs

"Heir of the Puritans"

I am persuaded that the use of a good Catechism in all our families will be a great safeguard against the increasing errors of the times, and therefore I have compiled this little manual from the Westminster Assembly's and Baptist Catechisms, for the use of my own church and congregation. Those who use it in their families or classes must labour to explain the sense; but the words should be carefully learned by heart, for they will be understood better as years pass.

May the Lord bless my dear friends and their families evermore, is the prayer of their loving Pastor.

C. H. Spurgeon

* * * * *

Study to shew thyself approved unto God, a workman that needeth not to be ashamed, rightly dividing the word of truth (2 Tim. 2:15)

* * * * *

Questions

1. What is the chief end of man?
2. What rule has God given to direct us how we may glorify him?
3. What do the Scriptures principally teach?
4. What is God?
5. Are there more Gods than one?
6. How many persons are there in the Godhead?
7. What are the decrees of God?
8. How does God execute his decrees?
9. What is the work of creation?
10. How did God create man?
11. What are God's works of providence?
12. What special act of providence did God exercise toward man in the state wherein he was created?
13. Did our parents continue in the state wherein they were created?
14. What is sin?
15. Did all mankind fall in Adam's first transgression?
16. Into what estate did the fall bring mankind?
17. Wherein consists the sinfulness of that state whereinto man fell?
18. What is the misery of that state whereinto man fell?
19. Did God leave all mankind to perish in the state of sin and misery?
20. Who is the Redeemer of God's elect?
21. How did Christ, being the Son of God, become man?
22. What offices does Christ execute as our Redeemer?
23. How does Christ execute the office of a prophet?
24. How does Christ execute the office of a priest?
25. How does Christ execute the office of a king?
26. Wherein did Christ's humiliation consist?
27. Wherein consists Christ's exaltation?
28. How are we made partakers of the redemption purchased by Christ?
29. How does the Spirit apply to us the redemption purchased by Christ?
30. What is effectual calling?
31. What benefits do they who are effectually called, partake of in this life?

32. What is justification?
33. What is adoption?
34. What is sanctification?
35. What are the benefits which in this life do either accompany or flow from justification, adoption, and sanctification?
36. What benefits do believers receive from Christ at their death?
37. What benefits do believers receive from Christ at the resurrection?
38. What shall be done to the wicked at their death?
39. What shall be done to the wicked at the day of judgment?
40. What did God reveal to man for the rule of his obedience?
41. What is the sum of the ten commandments?
42. Which is the first commandment?
43. What is required in the first commandment?
44. Which is the second commandment?
45. What is required in the second commandment?
46. What is forbidden in the second commandment?
47. Which is the third commandment?
48. What is required in the third commandment?
49. Which is the fourth commandment?
50. What is required in the fourth commandment?
51. How is the Sabbath to be sanctified?
52. Which is the fifth commandment?
53. What is required in the fifth commandment?
54. What is the reason annexed to the fifth commandment?
55. Which is the sixth commandment?
56. What is forbidden in the sixth commandment?
57. Which is the seventh commandment?
58. What is forbidden in the seventh commandment?
59. Which is the eighth commandment?
60. What is forbidden in the eighth commandment?
61. Which is the ninth commandment?
62. What is required in the ninth commandment?
63. Which is the tenth commandment?
64. What is forbidden in the tenth commandment?
65. Is any man able perfectly to keep the commandments of God?
66. Are all transgressions of the law equally heinous?
67. What does every sin deserve?
68. How may we escape his wrath and curse due to us for sin?

69. What is faith in Jesus Christ?

70. What is repentance to life?

71. What are the outward means whereby the Holy Spirit communicates to us the benefits of redemption?

72. How is the Word made effectual to salvation?

73. How is the Word to be read and heard that it may become effectual to salvation?

74. How do Baptism and the Lord's Supper become spiritually helpful?

75. What is baptism?

76. To whom is Baptism to be administered?

77. Are the infants of such as are professing believers to be baptised?

78. How is baptism rightly administered?

79. What is the duty of such as are rightly baptised?

80. What is the Lord's Supper?

81. What is required to the worthy receiving of the Lord's Supper?

82. What is meant by the words, "until he come," which are used by the apostle Paul in reference to the the Lord's Supper?

* * * * *

Questions and Answers *(with proofs)*

1. Q. What is the chief end of man?
   . A. Man's chief end is to glorify God (1 Cor. 10:31), and to enjoy him for ever (Ps. 73:25-26).

2. Q. What rule has God given to direct us how we may glorify him?
   . A. The Word of God which is contained in the Scriptures of the Old and New Testaments (Eph. 2:20; 2 Tim. 3:16) is the only rule to direct us how we may glorify God and enjoy him (1 Jn. 1:3).

3. Q. What do the Scriptures principally teach?
   . A. The Scriptures principally teach what man is to believe concerning God, and what duty God requires of man (2 Tim. 1:13; Eccl. 12:13).

4. Q. What is God?
  . A. God is Spirit (Jn. 4:24), infinite (Job 11:7), eternal (Ps.
        90:2; 1 Tim. 1:17), and unchangeable (Jas. 1:17) in his
        being (Exod. 3:14), wisdom, power (Ps. 147:5), holiness
        (Rev. 4:8), justice, goodness and truth (Exod. 34:6-7).

* * * * *

5. Q. Are there more Gods than one?
  . A. There is but one only (Deut. 6:4), the living and true God
        (Jer. 10:10).

* * * * *

6. Q. How many persons are there in the Godhead?
  . A. There are three persons in the Godhead, the Father, the
        Son, and the Holy Spirit, and these three are one God, the
        same in essence, equal in power and glory (1 Jn. 5:7; Matt.
        28:19).

* * * * *

7. Q. What are the decrees of God?
  . A. The decrees of God are his eternal purpose according to
        the counsel of his own will, whereby for his own glory he
        has foreordained whatever comes to pass (Eph. 1:11-12).

* * * * *

8. Q. How does God execute his decrees?
  . A. God executes his decrees in the works of creation (Rev.
        4:11), and providence (Dan. 4:35).

* * * * *

9. Q. What is the work of creation?
  . A. The work of creation is God's making all things (Gen.
        1:1) of nothing, by the Word of his power (Heb. 11:3),
        in six normal consecutive days (Exod. 20:11), and all
        very good (Gen. 1:31).

* * * * *

10. Q. How did God create man?
    A. God created man, male and female, after his own image (Gen. 1:27), in knowledge, righteousness, and holiness (Col 3:10; Eph. 4:24) with dominion over the creatures (Gen. 1:28).

* * * * *

11. Q. What are God's works of providence?
    A. God's works of providence are his most holy (Ps. 145:17), wise, (Isa. 28:29) and powerful (Heb. 1:3), preserving and governing all his creatures, and all their actions (Ps. 103:19; Matt. 10:29).

* * * * *

12. Q. What special act of providence did God exercise toward man in the state wherein he was created?
    A. When God had created man, he entered into a covenant of life with him, upon condition of perfect obedience; (Gal. 3:12) forbidding him to eat of the tree of the knowledge of good and evil, upon pain of death. (Gen. 2:17)

* * * * *

13. Q. Did our first parents continue in the state wherein they were created?
    A. Our first parents being left to the freedom of their own will, fell from the state wherein they were created, by sinning against God, (Eccl. 7:29) by eating the forbidden fruit (Gen. 3:6-8).

* * * * *

14. Q. What is sin?
    A. Sin is any want of conformity to, or transgression of the law of God (1 Jn. 3:4).

* * * * *

15. Q. Did all mankind fall in Adam's first transgression?
    A. The covenant being made with Adam, not only for himself but for his posterity, all mankind descending from him by

ordinary generation, sinned in him, and fell with him in his first transgression (1 Cor. 15:22; Rom. 5:12).

* * * * *

16. Q. Into what estate did the fall bring mankind?
 . A. The fall brought mankind into a state of sin and misery (Rom. 5:18).

* * * * *

17. Q. Wherein consists the sinfulness of that state whereinto man fell?
 . A. The sinfulness of that state whereinto man fell, consists in the guilt of Adam's first sin (Rom. 5:19), the want of original righteousness, (Rom. 3:10) and the corruption of his whole nature, which is commonly called original sin (Eph. 2:1; Ps. 51:5), together with all actual transgressions which proceed from it (Matt. 15:19).

* * * * *

18. Q. What is the misery of that state whereinto man fell?
 . A. All mankind, by their fall, lost communion with God (Gen. 3:8, 24), are under his wrath and curse (Eph. 2:3; Gal. 3:10), and so made liable to all the miseries in this life, to death itself, and to the pains of hell for ever (Rom. 6:23; Matt. 25:41).

* * * * *

19. Q. Did God leave all mankind to perish in the state of sin and misery?
 . A. God having, out of his good pleasure from all eternity, elected some to everlasting life (2 Thess. 2:13), did enter into a covenant of grace to deliver them out of the state of sin and misery, and to bring them into a state of salvation by a Redeemer (Rom. 5:21).

* * * * *

20. Q. Who is the Redeemer of God's elect?

A. The only Redeemer of God's elect is the Lord Jesus Christ (1 Tim. 2:5), who being the eternal Son of God, became man (Jn. 1:14), and so was and continues to be God and man, in two distinct natures and one person for ever (1 Tim. 3:16; Col. 2:9).

* * * * *

21. Q. How did Christ, being the Son of God, become man?

A. Christ, the son of God, became man by taking to himself a true body (Heb. 2:14), and a reasonable soul (Matt. 26:38; Heb. 4:15), being conceived by the power of the Holy Spirit in the Virgin Mary, and born of her (Lk. 1:31, 35), yet without sin (Heb. 7:26).

* * * * *

22. Q. What offices does Christ execute as our Redeemer?

A. Christ as our Redeemer executes the offices of a prophet (Acts 3:22), of a priest (Heb. 5:6), and of a king (Ps. 2:6), both in his state of humiliation and exaltation.

* * * * *

23. Q. How does Christ execute the office of a prophet?

A. Christ executes the office of a prophet, in revealing to us (Jn. 1:18), by his Word (Jn. 20:31), and Spirit (Jn. 14:26), the will of God for our salvation.

* * * * *

24. Q. How does Christ execute the office of a priest?

A. Christ executes the office of a priest, in his once offering up himself a sacrifice to satisfy divine justice (Heb. 9:28), and to reconcile us to God (Heb. 2:17), and in making continual intercession for us (Heb. 7:25).

* * * * *

25. Q. How does Christ execute the office of a king?

A. Christ executes the office of a king in subduing us to himself, (Ps. 110:3) in ruling and defending us (Matt. 2:6;

1 Cor. 15:25), and in restraining and conquering all his and our enemies.

* * * * *

26. Q. Wherein did Christ's humiliation consist?

.   A. Christ's humiliation consisted in his being born, and that in a low condition (Lk. 2:7), made under the law (Gal. 4:4), undergoing the miseries of this life (Isa. 53:3), the wrath of God (Matt. 27:46), and the cursed death of the cross; (Phil. 2:8) in being buried, and continuing under the power of death for a time (Matt. 12:40).

* * * * *

27. Q. Wherein consists Christ's exaltation?

.   A. Christ's exaltation consists in his rising again from the dead on the third day (1 Cor. 15:4), in ascending up into heaven, and sitting at the right hand of God the Father (Mk. 16:19), and in coming to judge the world at the last day (Acts 17:31).

* * * * *

28. Q. How are we made partakers of the redemption purchased by Christ?

.   A. We are made partakers of the redemption purchased by Christ, by the effectual application of it to us (Jn. 1:12) by his Holy Spirit. (Tit. 3:5-6)

* * * * *

29. Q. How does the Spirit apply to us the redemption purchased by Christ?

.   A. The Spirit applies to us the redemption purchased by Christ, by working faith in us (Eph. 2:8), and by it uniting us to Christ in our effectual calling (Eph. 3:17).

* * * * *

30. Q. What is effectual calling?

.   A. Effectual calling is the work of God's Spirit (2 Tim. 1:9) whereby, convincing us of our sin and misery (Acts 2:37), enlightening our minds in the knowledge of Christ (Acts 26:18), and renewing our wills (Ezek. 36:26), he does persuade and enable us to embrace Jesus Christ freely offered to us in the gospel (Jn. 6:44-45).

* * * * *

31. Q. What benefits do they who are effectually called, partake of in this life?

. A. They who are effectually called, do in this life partake of justification (Rom. 8:30), adoption (Eph. 1:5), sanctification, and the various benefits which in this life do either accompany, or flow from them (1 Cor. 1:30).

* * * * *

32. Q. What is justification?

. A. Justification is an act of God's free grace, wherein he pardons all our sins (Rom. 3:24; Eph. 1:7), and accepts us as righteous in his sight (2 Cor. 5:21) only for the righteousness of Christ imputed to us (Rom. 5:19), and received by faith alone (Gal. 2:16; Phil. 3:9).

* * * * *

33. Q. What is adoption?

. A. Adoption is an act of God's free grace (1 Jn. 3:1), whereby we are received into the number, and have a right to all the privileges of the sons of God (Jn. 1:12; Rom. 8:17).

* * * * *

34. Q. What is sanctification?

. A. Sanctification is the work of God's Spirit (2 Thess. 2:13), whereby we are renewed in the whole man after the image of God (Eph. 4:24), and are enabled more and more to die to sin, and live to righteousness (Rom. 6:11).

* * * * *

35. Q. What are the benefits which in this life do either accompany or flow from justification, adoption, and sanctification?

A. The benefits which in this life do accompany or flow from
    justification (Rom. 5:1-2, 5), are assurance of God's love,
    peace of conscience, joy in the Holy Spirit (Rom. 14:17),
    increase of grace, perseverance in it to the end (Prov. 4:18;
    1 Jn. 5:13; 1 Pet. 1:5).

                    * * * * *

36. Q. What benefits do believers receive from Christ at their
        death?
A. The souls of believers are at their death made perfect in
    holiness (Heb. 12:23 and do immediately pass into glory,
    (Phil. 1:23; 2 Cor. 5:8; Lk. 23:43), and their bodies, being
    still united to Christ (1 Thess. 4:14), do rest in their graves
    (Isa. 57:2) till the resurrection (Job 19:26).

                    * * * * *

37. Q. What benefits do believers receive from Christ at the
        resurrection?
A. At the resurrection, believers being raised up in glory (1
    Cor. 15:43), shall be openly acknowledged and acquitted
    in the day of judgment (Matt. 10:32), and made perfectly
    blessed both in soul and body in the full enjoying of God
    (1 Jn. 3:2) to all eternity (1 Thess. 4:17).

                    * * * * *

38. Q. What shall be done to the wicked at their death?
A. The souls of the wicked shall at their death be cast into
    the torments of hell (Lk. 16:22-24), and their bodies lie
    in their graves till the resurrection, and judgement of the
    great day (Ps. 49:14).

                    * * * * *

39. Q. What shall be done to the wicked at the day of judgment?
A. At the day of judgment the bodies of the wicked being
    raised out of their graves, shall be sentenced, together
    with their souls, to unspeakable torments with the devil
    and his angels for ever (Dan. 12:2; Jn. 5:28-29; 2 Thess.
    1:9; Matt. 25:41).

* * * * *

40. Q. What did God reveal to man for the rule of his obedience?
  . A. The rule which God first revealed to man for his obedience, is the moral law (Deut. 10:4; Matt. 19:17), which is summarised in the ten commandments.

* * * * *

41. Q. What is the sum of the ten commandments?
  . A. The sum of the ten commandments is to love the Lord our God with all our heart, with all our soul, with all our strength, and with all our mind; and our neighbour as ourselves (Matt. 22:37-40).

* * * * *

42. Q. Which is the first commandment?
  . A. The first commandment is, "Thou shalt have no other gods before me."

* * * * *

43. Q. What is required in the first commandment?
  . A. The first commandment requires us to know (1 Chron. 28:9) and acknowledge God to be the only true God, and our God (Deut. 26:17), and to worship and glorify him accordingly (Matt. 4:10).

* * * * *

44. Q. Which is the second commandment?
  . A. The second commandment is, "Thou shalt not make unto thee any graven image, or any likeness of any thing that is in heaven above, or that is in the earth beneath, or that is in the water under the earth: Thou shalt not bow down thyself to them, nor serve them: for I the Lord thy God am a jealous God, visiting the iniquity of the fathers upon the children unto the third and fourth generation of them that hate me; and shewing mercy unto thousands of them that love me, and keep my commandments."

* * * * *

45. Q. What is required in the second commandment?

. A. The second commandment requires the receiving, observing (Deut. 32:46; Matt. 28:20), and keeping pure and entire all such religious worship and ordinances as God has appointed in his Word (Deut. 12:32).

* * * * *

46. Q. What is forbidden in the second commandment?

. A. The second commandment forbids the worshipping of God by images, (Deut. 4:15-16) or any other way not appointed in his Word (Col. 2:18).

* * * * *

47. Q. Which is the third commandment?

. A. The third commandment is, "Thou shalt not take the name of the Lord thy God in vain; for the Lord will not hold him guiltless that takes his name in vain."

* * * * *

48. Q. What is required in the third commandment?

. A. The third commandment requires the holy and reverent use of God's names (Ps. 29:2), titles, attributes (Rev. 15:3-4), ordinances (Eccl. 5:1), Word (Ps. 138:2), and works (Job 36:24; Deut. 28:58-59).

* * * * *

49. Q. Which is the fourth commandment?

. A. The fourth commandment is, "Remember the Sabbath day, to keep it holy. Six days shalt thou labour, and do all thy work: but the seventh day is the Sabbath of the Lord thy God: in it thou shalt not do any work, thou, nor thy son, nor thy daughter, thy manservant, nor thy maidservant, nor they cattle, nor thy stranger that is within thy gates. For in six days the Lord made heaven and earth, the sea, and all that in them is, and rested the seventh day: wherefore the Lord blessed the Sabbath day and hallowed it."

* * * * *

50. Q. What is required in the fourth commandment?
  . A. The fourth commandment requires the keeping holy to God such set times as he has appointed in his Word, expressly one whole day in seven, to be a holy Sabbath to himself (Lev. 19:30; Deut. 5:12).

* * * * *

51. Q. How is the Sabbath to be sanctified?
  . A. The Sabbath is to be sanctified by a holy resting all that day, even from such worldly employments and recreations as are lawful on other days (Lev. 23:3), and spending the whole time in the public and private exercises of God's worship (Ps. 92:1-2; Isa. 58:13-14), except so much as is taken up in the works of necessity and mercy (Matt. 12:11-12).

* * * * *

52. Q. Which is the fifth commandment?
  . A. The fifth commandment is, "Honour thy father and thy mother: that thy days may be long upon the land which the Lord thy God giveth thee."

* * * * *

53. Q. What is required in the fifth commandment?
  . A. The fifth commandment requires the preserving the honour, and performing the duties belonging to every one in their various positions and relationships as superiors (Eph. 5:21-22; Eph. 6:1, 5; Rom. 13:1), inferiors (Eph. 6:9), or equals (Rom. 12:10).

* * * * *

54. Q. What is the reason annexed to the fifth commandment?
  . A. The reason annexed to the fifth commandment is, a promise of long life and prosperity—as far as it shall serve for God's glory, and their own good—to all such as keep this commandment (Eph. 6:2-3).

* * * * *

55. Q. Which is the sixth commandment?
. A. The sixth commandment is, "Thou shalt not kill."

* * * * *

56. Q. What is forbidden in the sixth commandment?
. A. The sixth commandment forbids the taking away of our own life (Acts 16:28), or the life of our neighbour unjustly (Gen. 9:6), or whatever tends to it (Prov. 24:11-12).

* * * * *

57. Q. Which is the seventh commandment?
. A. The seventh commandment is, "Thou shalt not commit adultery."

* * * * *

58. Q. What is forbidden in the seventh commandment?
. A. The seventh commandment forbids all unchaste thoughts (Matt. 5:28; Col. 4:6), words (Eph. 5:4; 2 Tim. 2:22), and actions (Eph. 5:3).

* * * * *

59. Q. Which is the eighth commandment?
. A. The eighth commandment is, "Thou shalt not steal."

* * * * *

60. Q. What is forbidden in the eighth commandment?
. A. The eighth commandment forbids whatever does or may unjustly hinder our own (1 Tim. 5:8; Prov. 28:19; Prov. 21:6), or our neighbour's wealth, or outward estate (Eph. 4:28).

* * * * *

61. Q. Which is the ninth commandment?
. A. The ninth commandment is, "Thou shalt not bear false witness against thy neighbour."

* * * * *

62. Q. What is required in the ninth commandment?
. A. The ninth commandment requires the maintaining and promoting of truth between man and man (Zech. 8:16), and of our own (1 Pet. 3:16; Acts 25:10), and our neighbour's good name (3 Jn. 1:12), especially in witness-bearing (Prov. 14:5, 25).

* * * * *

63. Q. What is the tenth commandment?
. A. The tenth commandment is, "Thou shalt not covet thy neighbour's house; thou shalt not covet thy neighbour's wife, nor his manservant, or his maidservant, nor his ox, nor his ass, nor anything that is thy neighbour's."

* * * * *

64. Q. What is forbidden in the tenth commandment?
. A. The tenth commandment forbids all discontentment with our own estate (1 Cor. 10:10), envying or grieving at the good of our neighbour, (Gal. 5:26) and all inordinate emotions and affections to anything that is his (Col. 3:5).

* * * * *

65. Q. Is any man able perfectly to keep the commandments of God?
. A. No mere man, since the fall, is able in his life perfectly to keep the commandments of God (Eccl. 7:20), but does daily break them in thought, (Gen. 8:21) word (Jas. 3:8), and deed (Jas. 3:2).

* * * * *

66. Q. Are all transgressions of the law equally heinous?
. A. Some sins in themselves, and by reason of various aggravations, are more heinous in the sight of God than others (Jn. 19:11; 1 Jn. 5:15).

* * * * *

67. Q. What does every sin deserve?
. A. Every sin deserves God's wrath and curse, both in this life and that which is to come (Eph. 5:6; Ps. 11:6).

* * * * *

68. Q. How may we escape his wrath and curse due to us for sin?
. A. To escape the wrath and curse of God due to us for sin, we must believe in the Lord Jesus Christ (Jn. 3:16), trusting alone to his blood and righteousness. This faith is attended by repentance for the past (Acts 20:21) and leads to holiness in the future.

* * * * *

69. Q. What is faith in Jesus Christ?
. A. Faith in Jesus Christ is a saving grace (Heb. 10:39), whereby we receive (Jn. 1:12), and rest upon him alone for salvation (Phil. 3:9), as he is set forth in the gospel (Isa. 33:22).

* * * * *

70. Q. What is repentance to life?
. A. Repentance to life is a saving grace (Acts 11:18), whereby a sinner, out of a true sense of his sins (Acts 2:37), and apprehension of the mercy of God in Christ (Joel 2:13), does with grief and hatred of his sin turn from it to God (Jer. 31:18-19), with full purpose to strive after new obedience (Ps. 119:59).

* * * * *

71. Q. What are the outward means whereby the Holy Spirit communicates to us the benefits of redemption?
. A. The outward and ordinary means whereby the Holy Spirit communicates to us the benefits of Christ's redemption, are the Word, by which souls are begotten to spiritual life; Baptism, the Lord's Supper, Prayer, and Meditation, by all which believers are further edified in their most holy faith (Acts 2:41-42; Jas. 1:18).

* * * * *

72. Q. How is the Word made effectual to salvation?

. A. The Spirit of God makes the reading, but especially the preaching of the Word, an effectual means of convicting and converting sinners, (Ps. 19:7) and of building them up in holiness and comfort (1 Thess. 1:6), through faith to salvation (Rom. 1:16).

* * * * *

73. Q. How is the Word to be read and heard that it may become effectual to salvation?

. A. That the Word may become effectual to salvation, we must attend to it with diligence (Prov. 8:34), preparation (1 Pet. 2:1-2), and prayer (Ps 119:18), receive it with faith (Heb. 4:2), and love (2 Thess. 2:10), lay it up into our hearts (Ps. 119:11), and practise it in our lives (Jas. 1:25).

* * * * *

74. Q. How do Baptism and the Lord's Supper become spiritually helpful?

. A. Baptism and the Lord's Supper become spiritually helpful, not from any virtue in them, or in him who does administer them (1 Cor. 3:7; 1 Pet. 3:21), but only by the blessing of Christ (1 Cor. 3:6), and the working of the Spirit in those who by faith receive them (1 Cor. 12:13).

* * * * *

75. Q. What is Baptism?

. A. Baptism is an ordinance of the New Testament, instituted by Jesus Christ (Matt. 28:19), to be to the person baptised a sign of his fellowship with him, in his death, and burial, and resurrection (Rom. 6:3; Col. 2:12), of his being ingrafted into him (Gal. 3:27), of remission of sins (Mk. 1:4; Acts 22:16), and of his giving up himself to God through Jesus Christ, to live and walk in newness of life (Rom. 6:4-5).

* * * * *

76. Q. To whom is Baptism to be administered?

. A. Baptism is to be administered to all those who actually profess repentance towards God (Acts 2:38; Matt. 3:6; Mk. 16:16; Acts 8:12, 36-37; Acts 10:47-48), and faith in our Lord Jesus Christ, and to none other.

* * * * *

77. Q. Are the infants of such as are professing to be baptised?

. A. The infants of such as are professing believers are not to be baptised, because there is neither command nor example in the Holy Scriptures for their baptism (Exod. 23:13; Prov. 30:6).

* * * * *

78. Q. How is baptism rightly administered?

. A. Baptism is rightly administered by immersion, or dipping the whole body of the person in water (Matt. 3:16; Jn. 3:23), in the name of the Father, and of the Son, and of the Holy Spirit, according to Christ's institution, and the practice of the apostles (Matt. 28:19-20), and not by sprinkling or pouring of water, or dipping some part of the body, after the tradition of men (Jn. 4:1-2; Acts 8:38-39).

* * * * *

79. Q. What is the duty of such as are rightly baptized?

. A. It is the duty of such as are rightly baptized, to give up themselves to some particular and orderly Church of Jesus Christ (Acts 2:47; 9:26; 1 Pet. 2:5), that they may walk in all the commandments and ordinances of the Lord blameless (Lk. 1:6).

* * * * *

80. Q. What is the Lord's Supper?

. A. The Lord's Supper is an ordinance of the New Testament, instituted by Jesus Christ; wherein, by giving and receiving bread and wine, according to his appointment, his death is shown forth (1 Cor. 11:23-26), and the worthy receivers are, not after a corporeal and carnal manner, but by faith, made partakers of his body and blood, with all his benefits, to their spiritual nourishment, and growth in grace (1 Cor. 10:16).

* * * * *

81. Q. What is required to the worthy receiving of the Lord's Supper?

A. It is required of them who would worthily partake of the Lord's Supper, that they examine themselves of their knowledge to discern the Lord's body (1 Cor. 11:28-29), of their faith to feed upon him (2 Cor. 13:5), of their repentance (1 Cor. 11:31), love (1 Cor. 11:18-20), and new obedience, (1 Cor. 5:8) lest coming unworthily, they eat and drink judgment to themselves (1 Cor. 11:27-29).

* * * * *

82. Q. What is meant by the words, "until he come," which are used by the apostle Paul in reference to the Lord's Supper?

A. They plainly teach us that our Lord Jesus Christ will come a second time; which is the joy and hope of all believers (Acts 1:11 1 Thess. 4:16).

A TRAVELLER'S LETTERS HOME

Chapter 73

STANDING WHERE Satan's seat is, in the midst of ten thousand idols, I beseech those who worship God in the spirit to wrestle in prayer for times of refreshing, that all lands may know that Jesus Christ is Lord. How long shall the Name of Jesus be blasphemed by the idolatries of Antichrist? It maybe that the times of darkness will last till the children of light cry out bitterly, day and night, by reason of soul-anguish. Then will God avenge His own elect, and that speedily. As I have trodden the Appian Way, I have rejoiced that Jesus, whom Paul preached, is yet alive, and is certain, in due season, to put down His enemies. Already He has desolated the Colosseum, where His faithful martyrs poured forth their blood; the pagan power has fallen, and so also shall the papal, and all other which opposes His Kingdom. Let us proclaim a spiritual crusade, and set up our banners by redoubled prayer. It is certain that supplication produces marvelous results in Heaven and earth; its power is proven in our own personal experience, and throughout the history of the Church. Brethren, LET US PRAY.—C. H. S., *in letter from Rome, to Tabernacle church and friends in general*

INTRODUCTION, BY MRS. C. H. SPURGEON.

IN 1868, my travelling days were done. Henceforth, for many years, I was a prisoner in a sick-chamber, and my beloved had to leave me when the strain of his many labors and responsibilities compelled him to seek rest far away from home. These separations were very painful to hearts so tenderly united as were ours, but we each bore our share of the sorrow as heroically as we could, and softened it as far as possible by constant correspondence. "God bless you," he wrote once, "and help you to bear my absence. Better that I should be away well, than at home suffering,—better to your loving heart, I know. Do not fancy, even for a moment, that absence could make our hearts colder to each other; our attachment is now a perfect union, indissoluble for ever. My sense of your value, and experience of your goodness, are now united to the deep passion of love which was there at the first alone. Every year casts out another anchor to hold me even more firmly to you, though none was needed even from the first. May my own Lord, whose chastening hand has necessitated this absence, give you a secret inward recompense in soul, and also, another recompense in the healing of the body! All my heart remains in your keeping."

It is marvelous to me, as I survey the yearly packets of letters which are now such precious treasures, how my husband could have managed, amidst the bustle and excitement, of foreign travel, to have written so much and so often. I many times begged him to spare himself in this matter, but he constantly assured me that it delighted him to do it; he said "Every word I write is a pleasure to me, as much as ever it can be to you; it is only a lot of odds and ends I send you, but I put them down as they come, so that you may see it costs me no labor, but is just a happy scribble. Don't fret because I write you so many letters, it is such a pleasure to tell out my joy." Every day his dear messages came to me, except, of course, when a long railway journey intervened;—and, sometimes, as an unexpected gladness, he would post two in one day, that I might be comforted concerning him. On an important tour, like the one recorded in the following chapters, the letters would be illustrated by many amusing pen-and-ink sketches, of people, costumes, landscapes, trees, wells, or anything which particularly struck him. Plans of the rooms he occupied in the various hotels were very frequent, and enabled me better to imagine the comfort or otherwise of his surroundings. At one house at Nice, there was a delightful little platform or terrace opening out of his bedroom, and of this he sent a most elaborate sketch, so that I might share his pleasure in such an unusual addition to a sleeping apartment. "I am like Peter on the housetop," he wrote, "and though no sheet is let down to me, yet have I learned much that the sheet taught the apostle, and I count nothing common or unclean, no view unhallowed, no scenery to be avoided lest it should turn me away from communion with God. He has sanctified sea and mountain, housetop and street to me; and when my heart is devout, all these are helps and not hindrances to fellowship with Himself. I can little sympathize with those ultra-spiritually-minded people, who are so unspiritual that only the closed eye can enable them to think of their God."

I have said that the letters were "illustrated," but I think *illuminated* would be a better word to use; for, looking at them after these many years, with overflowing eyes, the little sketches seem to bear a rainbow light within them, and to sparkle with colors which only a devoted love could have blended. They remind me of the patient care bestowed upon the Psalters and Missals of the Middle Ages, when the hand of some pious man toiled day after day to decorate the vellum pages,—simply to prove the love of his heart, and witness to the truth of his devotion. My beloved himself must have entertained some such feeling; for, at the end of a series of droll representations of women's head-gear which he had noticed in the streets of Botzen, he thus writes, "Now, sweetheart, may these trifles amuse you; *I count it a holy work to draw them,* if they cause you but one happy smile." That I smiled on them then, and weep over them now, is but a natural consequence of the more complete separation which God has willed for us,—he, dwelling in the land of glory,—I, still tarrying amid the shadow; of earth;—but I verily believe that, when I join him, "beyond the smiling and the weeping," there will be tender remembrances of all these details of earthly love, and of the plenitude of blessing which it garnered in our united lives. Surely we shall talk of all these things, in the pauses of adoring worship and of joyful service. There must be sweet converse in Heaven between those who loved, and suffered, and served together here below. Next to the rapture of seeing the King in His beauty, and beholding the face of Him who redeemed us to God by His blood, must be the happiness of the communion of saints, in that place of inconceivable blessedness which God has prepared for them that love Him. As Bishop Bickersteth finely puts it, in his description of Heaven,—

> "Every sight and sound
> Ravished the sense: and every loving heart
> Reflected joy to joy, and light to light,
> Like crystals in a cave flashing with fire,
> And multiplied our bliss a million-fold."

The two following chapters consist of extracts from the daily letters of my husband during his holiday journey to Rome, Naples, and Pompeii. I have given them *verbatim*, only withholding allusions to domestic concerns and personal matters, and condensing to a minimum the sweet love-talk which in great measure helped me to bear the pain of these, separations. I have almost grudged to do this; it has been a grief to fold up his precious words and hide their rare beauty from other eyes, for they shed so lovely a light upon his character; but, in many instances, they were too sacred to be reproduced. Every here and there, I have allowed a sentence or two to reveal a glimpse of his great, tender, and true heart, as nothing else could have done; but the rest I have locked up again in the secret chambers of my memory.

The letters themselves are not set forth as examples of elegant style or well-rounded periods, or even of graceful phraseology; they are simply a loving husband's daily notes, to his sick wife, a record of his journeyings gladly and faithfully persevered in with the sole object of pleasing her, and relieving her sorrowful loneliness.

I hope they may interest many, and even instruct some. Recent tourists in Italy's classic clime will be pleasantly reminded of their own travels, and be able to trace the progress that has been made during the past twenty-five years in the great work of excavating old Rome, and the buried cities on the Mediterranean shore; and all who read them will, I trust, feel with me that they are worthily enshrined in these pages, which will bear witness to his spotless, beautiful life "till the day dawn, and the shadows flee away."

EXTRACTS FROM MY HUSBAND'S LETTERS.

Our party met punctually at Victoria, and our journey to Dover consisted of parentheses of sunshine and paragraphs of mist. The woods look as if they were expiring amid the tears of nature. The sea was not like either sort of the prophet's figs, but was inclined to be irritable without having vigor enough to work itself into actual passion. Many suffered much from the marine malady; and, though we escaped it, yet we were glad to be again on the land which was meant for man; the sea is evidently only designed for fishes and sailors. We were asked our names at Calais; and, having answered to that first question of the Catechism, we were allowed to tread the soil of Republican France. We were soon satisfactorily "restaurated", and en *route* for Brussels, *viâ* Lille, Tournay, etc. The whole land is like a neatly-kept garden, from which the tillers derive all the produce possible. We had a good journey, reached our hotel at six o'clock, dined, then walked down to the Arcade which you will remember, and are now in our rooms, cozy and comfortable. The weather is delicious;—bright, clear, and balmy;—no fires needed; in fact, I am too warmly clad. The atmosphere is dry and light, and gives me new life. It seems very selfish to be writing thus to my dear prisoner at home, yet she loves me so much that the surest way to make her happy is to prove that I am enjoying my holiday. All my love I send thee; may the everlasting arms encompass thee, even the arms of my God and thine!

We were up early, and walked to the Botanical Gardens, and then on to the Church of St. Gudule, with its wonderful painted windows, some of them most ancient, others modern, but exquisite. These last represent a Jew stealing consecrated wafers, while other Jews are sticking daggers into them for the purpose of making them bleed. To me, it does not seem worse to carve wafers than to eat them; but the difference between tweedledum and tweedledee is sometimes immense. We then drove to the *Musee Wiertz*, which I have before described to you. It is certainly a very wonderful display of one man's powers, and a singular combination of the playful and the terrible. We saw all, and then went to the Luxembourg Station to continue our journey, by Waterloo, to Namur. O "days of auld lang syne," how ye flashed before me, especially when we rode along by the Meuse and Huy to Liege, and thence to Chaudfontaine, Verviers, and Aix-la-Chapelle! Alas! my dearest bides at home; and I, like a lone knight, can but remember the ladye of my love, for she rides not at my side as aforetime! The journey was exquisite for weather, temperature, and scenery; but it was long, and we were very hungry; so, when we sat down to table at 7.30, it was with the serious resolution to be avenged for our long fast.

This morning, I was up at six o'clock, revising a sermon. It is now raining for the first time since we left home; and this is convenient, for it makes it easier to remain indoors at work. Thus far, all has gone well, and we are grateful. To love God when all is smooth and sweet, is but the love of swine who know their feeder. The true test is to be able to bless His smiting hand, and cry, "Though He slay me yet will I trust in Him." You, my darling, have been enabled to do this; and though the weary, weary pain bows you down, you will be able to possess your soul in patience even unto the end. The Lord will comfort you with His choice consolations in the day of your afflictions. Some of those well-ripened apples which housewives bring forth amid the chill, leafless days of winter, God hath in reserve for time; wherefore, be of good courage, my sweetheart!

It rained till we left Cologne yesterday, when we traveled to Mayence along the banks of the Rhine. The light was gone by 5.30, so that we saw nothing beyond Andernach; the sky was leaden, and the atmosphere hazy. The woods, however, were ablaze with autumn fires, and the tints were inexpressibly lovely;—alas! the loveliness of decay. We reached here at 8.30, had tea, then crossed the bridge of boats, and returning, went up into the skies to bed (alluding to the height of the hotel).

Munich.—Yesterday, we were on the railroad all day long. We left Mayence at 10.20, and did not reach this city till 9.30. The first part of the road was tame, then followed a chapter of forests with their matchless pomp of autumnal glory. Anon, we mounted uphill into glens and. Mountain-valleys, which were presently succeeded by a river, with towns growing like osiers on its banks. This must be a superb city, and I want to spend today in seeing it; but we are in a fix. The only train over the Brenner leaves here at eleven at night. Innsbruck is the town at the foot of the pass on this side, and the train reaches and leaves there at three o'clock in the morning. So, you see, if we go on a bit, we shall be no better off. To think of going over a pass in the dark, seems to me to be a willful blasphemy of nature, if not of nature's God! We must find out if it cannot, be managed otherwise than as a deed of darkness. We must have a carriage, if possible; and see the marvels of the mountains.

This is an artistic city in all ways, a certain Greek-art appearance strikes one everywhere; not a sham, but a real reproduction of antiquity. We have been to the Glyptothek, a fine museum of statuary; but, really, after one has seen a few thousand nude figures, one feels content without any more anatomical models in stone. Thence, we visited a large picture-gallery,—which I think almost equal to the Louvre,—full of masterpieces of most of the ancient schools. We have been into a marvelous basilica, with pillars of the richest marble, and a ceiling of golden mosaic; also to the cathedral, to see the tomb of a German Emperor, a boy of the olden time, who has a bronze memorial of the noblest fashion. Then we entered the studio of a renowned sculptor, and saw the plaster-casts, the stone being chiseled, and the finished statues,—very interesting this. There is enough left for two or three days' enjoyment, but we must have it; and I scarcely regret this, for the weather is very damp and depressing. After all inquiries, I find we are compelled to go tonight at 11 o'clock, and pursue our weary way over the pass in the dark. Horses would require two days, and the roads are said to be in bad condition. "What can't be cured, must be endured;" so I say, "Southward Ho! at any price." My heart flies to my wifey; I have just kissed my hand to her. God bless her! Loads of love I telegraph by the soul-wire.

The Brenner is passed. We had some very uncomfortable experiences; the first part of the way, the guard wanted a coupon from us about every hour, and at Kuffstein we were hauled out of our nest, marched into the Austrian custom-house, made to wait, shivering, about thirty minutes, and then packed into a poor seedy carriage, cold and miserable, to continue our journey. Botzen was reached at last, but we were all so weary that we were glad to go into our rooms to rest till dinner. Since then, we have walked round the old-fashioned town, and under its long-arched lines of shops. We have also heard service in the cathedral opposite to our hotel; and very fine was the music, and very quaint the sight of a great crowd in the dark, except where a few had candles to see to read their mass-books. Do you remember this old inn (Kaiser Krone), where Emperors and Popes have lodged? It is a singular building; our rooms are on the same floor as the *salle,* but we have to go up, and then down to them, I am weary, and am looking forward to tomorrow's rest.

Sabbath eve.—This has been a very gracious, happy, restful day. Did I but know that you are better, I don't think I should have more to wish, except your company. We had a delicious morning service together;—read Psalm 22, and sang, "Come, let us sing the song of songs," and "Where God doth dwell." It was indeed a season of refreshing. Then we saw a service at the cathedral. Large and devout congregations assemble here at each hour from five a.m. to five p.m. I have never seen any Romish place so well attended. Every person in the town seemed to go to one of the hourly services, and very attentive and earnest they appeared to be. We looked in several times, and twice heard a kind of litany in, German, by the whole congregation, led by a layman in common dress. It reminded me of a prayer-meeting after service, for mass was over, and the altar-lights were put out, and then prayer broke out among all the people. After dinner, we walked up a mountain's side in the bright sun's genial warmth, and what a view we had! Snowy Alps, and dark forests, and then, lower down, the meadows and the terraced vines, and lower yet, the plain of the Adige and its villages. Our path led us by a series of shrines, similar to those at Varallo, but smaller, and at the end of the path was a "Calvary." We had sweet communion together here, and great enjoyment of God's presence. I am so much better in mind; I feel more elastic, light, and clear of forebodings. I now expect good news from my darling, whereas before I have felt sure of gloomy tidings.

Hotel Barbesi, Venice.—God be thanked for even the twinkling stars of better news in the letter I have just received from your dear self! It has poured with rain all day; indeed, they say it has rained for three whole weeks in these parts. We left Botzen at six o'clock, driving through mist, cloud, and deluges above, and through wide, far-reaching floods upon either side. We only stayed two hours at Verona, but I had the joy of receiving your letter there. On to Venice, found it better, but still very bad and wet. Had a gondola. Our rooms are very good, but an evil smell pervades the place; whether it is the canals in general, or these rooms in particular, we cannot tell. A waiter, who has just come up, says it is the *tapis*, which is new; this is possible, but the nuisance is none the better for that. Alas! the rain changes all things, and. Venice looks sad in her sodden state. We must hope for improvement.

After a splendid night's rest, I awoke at six o'clock, full of good spirits, and revised a sermon. After breakfast, we had a gondola, and went along the Grand Canal.

IN A GONDOLA ON THE GRAND CANAL.

Glorious! About eleven, the tide turned, and rain began again, so we went to St. Mark's, and saw the grand old cathedral, which is the same as ever, but needs sunshine to perfect it. Thence to the Doge's Palace,—you know all the details of these places. The rain poured down when we got under the black cover of the gondola; but it was a delightful experience to be so sheltered, and yet to be moving through the floods.

ST. MARK'S CATHEDRAL, VENICE.

We went to the Jesuits' Church, that fine marble one in the poorer part of the city;—you remember the curtains and carpet all reproduced in marble. Then we explored a glass manufactory, this was very interesting; they make mosaics, and mirrors, and chandeliers of the fine Venice glass, very wonderful to look upon. Still it rained, and the water was over St. Mark's Square in front of the cathedral. Nevertheless, we visited Santa Maria Gloriosa, where is Canova's pyramidical tomb, and marble enough to stock a city; and then to Santa Maria del Salute, opposite to our hotel. I have seen all these before, yet was still very much interested.

It is pitiable to see the poor people look soaked and only half-alive. Only the pigeons of St. Mark's are gay; they fly as a cloud, and swarm on the windows, and even enter the rooms of the houses all round the square; one might almost tread on them, they are so tame. The unhappy vendors of shells and miniature gondolas will, I fear, be half-starved, and the flower-girls look very downhearted. The water now is over the parks, and up to the doors; yet Venice is not a bad place in wet weather, since you can keep dry in your gondola, and can look out through the windows.

6 a.m.—I awake grateful for another night's peaceful rest, only to find myself very badly bitten by mosquitoes. A mosquito is the most terrible of beasts. A lion delights in blood, but he does not suck it from living animals; he does not carefully prolong their tortures. A viper poisons, but he is generally content with one use of his fangs; but these small-winged serpents bite in scores of places in succession. My hands are a series of burning mountains. The creatures are as nearly omnipresent as Satan, which means that, though a mosquito cannot be everywhere, yet no mortal can be sure that he is not near him, or tell where he is not. Curtains are a delusion, pastilles are a snare; the little enemies are irritated by such attempts to escape their malice, and give you double punishment. O Italy! I have shed my blood for thy sake, and feel a love of thee (or something else) burning in my veins! The sooner I am away from thee, O fair Venice, the better, for thou dost deluge me by day, and devour me by night! I wonder how my two companions have fared; I shall go, by-and-by, and look for their remains! I have opened my windows, and the pests are pouring in, eager and hungry; but, as I am up and dressed, there will be no more of me available for them at present.

Today has been charming, and we have been in the gondola most of its lovely hours. The sights we saw were nothing compared with the delicious rowing in the city itself. Could you but have been there, it would have been as much of Paradise as this earth can ever yield. Venice decays, but her autumn is fair. The fear is, lest the "restorers" should come and deface her. We went to the Arsenal, but models of ships and guns would not interest you. Then to the Greek Church, and the Carmelites', and the Academy of Arts;—saw hosts of Madonnas and St. Sebastians, I am quite weary of them. The outside of Venice is *the* treat, the beauty, the enjoyment.

We are off tomorrow very early for Florence; the air is loaded with mosquitoes, and my hands are "a mask of sores," as Mrs. Gamp would say, and both Mr. Passmore and I suffer much. Venice cannot be endured with these torments.

We left Venice at 7.50, and proceeded to Bologna, which was reached by 12.10, after an uninteresting ride among perpetual trees festooned with vines,—muddy earth,—flooded fields,— and disconsolate maize-stalks. From 1.20 to 5 o'clock, we were traversing the mountains between Bologna and Pistoia, and a more marvelous road it has never been my lot to see. It was up, up, up, by the side of a torrent, which the rail crossed and recrossed, with rugged scenery of a sublime character on either hand. Then, in commencing the descent, we saw Pistoia, and the great plain of the Arno far below, like a raised map. It was a truly wonderful view, but was soon gone; and we rushed down zigzags, and saw it again, and lost it every few minutes. It is almost miraculous that a train can keep to the rails upon such descents. Down below at Pistoia, we found that the floods had done great damage; but the railway was all right, so we reached Florence about seven o'clock. All this is very uninteresting to read, but it was pleasant to experience, while good companionship and the sunshine made the whole journey enjoyable. Though wearied by the long hours of travelling, I an in every way more fresh and free from depression. May the Lord enrich me also in spiritual blessings, and send me back more capable of serving Him than I have ever been! We are off early tomorrow, so now, my darling, may God watch over thee, bless thee, and keep thee, and restore me to thee in joy and peace! Oceans of love, and as many kisses for you as the sand on the sea-shore. My next letter will be from "the city of the seven hills," if all is well.

"THE CITY OF THE SEVEN HILLS."

We are in Rome. Let a man say what he will, there is a thrill passes through his soul, at the thought of being in Rome, that he cannot experience anywhere else, except in the city of our Lord,— Jerusalem. There are interests and associations that cluster about "the eternal city" that a man must feel, if he has any soul at all. You remember that, last year, we started off for our first day's sight-seeing without a guide, and wandered about without knowing whither we went; this time, I can act as guide and interpreter, and am able to observe much which, on a former occasion, I had not noticed. Today, we went down the Corso, and up the Capitol.

THE CAPITOL, ROME

There are new excavations at its foot. We passed down the other side to the Forum, where they are still digging. Rome of the olden time is buried beneath itself, under its own ruins, and the Forum lies some ten, fifteen, and in some places thirty feet of earth below the present level. I soon found myself on what I knew to be the Via Sacra, along which the triumphal processions passed when the great generals returned from war, and climbed the Capitol in state; and it was a memorable thing to stand before the Arch of Titus, and gaze upon its bas-reliefs.

BAS-RELIEF ON THE ARCH OF TITUS, ROME.

There is Titus returning from the siege of Jerusalem, with the seven-branched golden candlestick, and the silver trumpets; and, while these things stand there, it is idle for infidels to say that the Bible is not true. It is good history. Nobody doubts what is written in stone upon the Arch of Titus, but the same story is found in the Book; and the more discoveries that are made of ancient cities, especially in Palestine, the more will the truth of the Book be confirmed, and the record upon stone will be found to tally with what is written on the tablets of God's Word.

Then we came to the Colosseum. What a place it is! Two-thirds of it are gone, and yet enough remains wherewith to build a great city! I climbed to the very top. Under an arch of one of the great corridors we sat down, and sang, "Am I a soldier of the cross?" "I'm not ashamed to own my Lord," and "Jesu's tremendous name;" and then I preached a little sermon from the text," Come, behold the works of the Lord, what desolations He hath made in the earth;" then we prayed, and sang, "Ashamed of Jesus?" just then, two persons went by, and said, in broad American, "Don't let us disturb you." To which I answered, "Come and join," but they replied, "Our time is too short," so we sang the Doxology, and went on. Pretty bold this, in such a public place, but very sweet to be remembered. "Boylston" rolled along the vaulted tunnels like a battle-song.

INTERIOR OF THE COLOSSEUM, ROME.

We went down to the Appian Way, and on to the baths of Titus. By a mistake, I took the party up a lane, and through the wrong gate; but, after all, this was fortunate, for it brought us to the top of the immense structure; and, looking down, we saw the rooms which before I had only seen from below, and this view gave us a better idea of their vastness and mystery. The building is a huge ruin, built upon a ruin. Nero had a golden palace here, but when Titus came into power, he buried it. Its roof was made of great arches, massive and strong, so he bored, holes through them, and poured in rubbish till the place was filled up, and then he built his baths on the top of all. *His* work is ruined; but now, part of the palace below has been dug out, and they have found gems of art, enough to fill hundreds of museums. Getting to the right entrance, we came across the custodian, an old wounded soldier, who showed us over the whole place, as far as practicable, telling us all he knew, pointing out every fresco, and putting a delightful zest into it for us all. It is a place of marvels! Its passages and rooms are countless, vast, weird, and most impressive; one could spend a week there, and then begin again. The excavations have brought to light treasures of porphyry, marble, and statues; and the paintings and frescoes of eighteen hundred years ago are as fresh as if they were painted yesterday. Your guide has a long pole, into which he screws another long pole with a lighted candle at the end, this he holds up as high as possible, and you see the paintings off the roof of Nero's palace. There are said to be two hundred rooms still unexcavated, and no one knows what treasures of art they may conceal. Strange to say, there is yet another house beneath this golden palace, for Nero built over the house of Mecaenas, the friend of Horace; and, after digging deep down, they have come to the mosaic pavements of the first structure erected on this extraordinary spot. I want a bigger head, to take all these wonders in, and hold my thoughts!

After all this, we went a little further, to the Palace of the Caesars, which is a mile and a-half round, and is being excavated. All is ruined, but it is so far opened up as to show the lower rooms, and the first, or Imperial floor. It consisted of many palaces, and would take a month to explore. In one part, I saw rooms just dug out, as fresh as when originally decorated, and remarkably like the Pompeian house in the Crystal Palace. There was Caesar's great hall, the place of his throne, the bath of the harem, the library, the academy or residence for philosophers, and the rooms for the Pretorian guard. In fact, the whole Palatine Hill is a palace; and as they dig down, they come to vast chambers and corridors which seem endless. One of these, quite as long as our Nightingale Lane, has its mosaic pavement all complete; we looked down from a great height upon it, and there were opened places far below that. The walls are usually even to ten feet thick, so the work must be very heavy. I should think all kinds of marble in the world can be picked up here; it is just a vast quarry! What heaps of broken wine-jars,— the champagne bottles of the Caesars! It is a mountain of ruins of porphyry, alabaster, and all precious things! From its top you see other great ruins of temples, basilicas, palaces, and theatres!

Then the guide said, "Now you must come and see the baths of Caracalla." I was bewildered, lost, confounded; but I went, and found a building more than a mile in length, which beat all we had seen before, and made me feel as if my senses would give way. These enormous baths could accommodate 1,600 persons at a time; they were in tiers, one for men, another for women, the third for slaves. There were hot baths, cold baths, steam baths, swimming baths; and all these were floored with mosaics which we saw uncovered as we stood there. The roof was destroyed by the Goths; and when it fell in, it smashed the floor; but here and there great portions—as big as our lawn—are left intact, and one could see the lovely patterns of the mosaic,—each room different. The huge brick walls still stand, but the marble facing is almost all gone. I think no living man can conceive what the place must have been in its glory. I needed to go to bed, to sleep off my stupor of wonder! I am foolish to try to write about it. It is like a tadpole describing a sea! The Farnese family have taken the fine statues and other treasures to Naples; but there are acres yet to be dug out, in which, doubtless, many more are buried, but it is too great an expense to dig away very fast.

ST. PETER'S, ROME.

I had one delicious half-hour during the day. I sat down alone opposite to St. Peter's, and felt as if in Elysium. The snow gone, the sun shining, and on the great obelisk I saw words which cheered my soul; they were these, "Christ conquers, Christ reigns, Christ rules, Christ defends His people from all evil." The Lord be praised; this is true, and the Pope and all the world shall know it! I love my love amidst all these great thoughts. She is my palace, my throne, my empress, my Rome, my world; yet I have more, my Savior, my Heaven! Bless you, my own!

Today is the Sabbath, and has been up till now most sweetly calm and happy. We had our little service, with breaking of bread, and the Lord was with us. I read a sermon, and our song and prayer were "in the spirit." May it please the Lord of peace to give the like holy rest to my beloved! We then walked on the Pincian, where there are few people during the day, but lovely groves, and beds of roses, with seats in every corner, and all Rome at one's feet. It was truly Sabbatic. All that nature and art can do, is to be seen in these gardens, where the loveliest statues look down upon you, and fountains ripple to tunes of peace, and aromatic trees breathe perfume. A statue of Jochebed laying Moses in his ark of bulrushes among the reeds, struck me as charming to the last degree. It stood as the center of a fountain., reeds and water-lilies grew at the rocky base, and the ripples of the little hidden jets made wavelets round the ark. Can you imagine it? Nothing in modern art has pleased me more,—perhaps nothing so much. This has been a blessed day to me, and I have been feeling so well; I almost tremble lest it should be too good to continue.

Another day of wonders! This morning, we drove to the great amphitheater of Marcellus, which once held 20,000 persons, and is far older than the Colosseum. It is buried for fourteen feet, and much built over and hidden; around it is a market for the poor, where I saw baskets full of cigar-ends which had no doubt been picked up in the street, and were being sold to be smoked in pipes. What would Marcellus have thought of this? Then we saw the long covered way which led from the theater to the baths of Agrippa,—a great colonnade, of which some pillars are visible, and others are built into the houses of the street which occupies its place. From thence to, the Jews' quarter, where the same use of old stones is apparent; capitals, friezes, cornices, and all sorts of marbles are let into the walls of the dwellings. Ah! the cruelties the Jews have suffered in that Ghetto, the barbarities which have there been inflicted upon God's ancient people! Their district is often flooded by the Tiber; and, on one occasion, when they made an appeal to the papal authorities, because their houses were ten or twelve feet under water, the only answer they received was that the water would do the Jews good! There was a law in Rome, only lately repealed, that a hundred men and fifty women from the Jewish quarter must go to the Church of St. Angelo every Sunday, and they were driven there with whips; and if one of them went to sleep, there was a whip to wake him up, that he might hear himself and his forefathers bitterly abused. On certain days of the Carnival, the Jews were obliged to run races in the Corso, stripped of almost all their clothing, and then the people showered execrations and curses upon them. Time would fail to tell of their sufferings and privations, besides which they were forced to pay large sums of money to their oppressors. Matters have mended somewhat lately, and they are relieved from many of the most cruel persecutions of former days; but they are oppressed still, and I was greatly moved when, in the Church in the Ghetto, I saw this message from the Lord plainly set forth before them, "All day long I have stretched forth My hands unto a disobedient and gainsaying people."

Today we went several miles along the Appian Way. What bliss ever to see it! On both sides, for many miles, it is skirted by tombs, temples, *columbaria,* and ruins of villas in continuous lines. It is a British Museum ten miles long! I felt a strange joy in walking along the same road which Paul trod, when the brethren from Rome came to meet him. From it can be seen Tusculum and Tivoli, and the long line of the Claudian aqueduct, on arches all the way from the mountains into Rome, as also the temple of Romulus, and the great circus of Maxentius. What a world of wonders! We went as far as the Casale Rotundo, a round tomb so large that, being full of rubbish, there's a house, and stables, and. an olive garden on the top. We wanted to investigate, so climbed up, and were rewarded by the sight of a family of very scantily-clothed children; their mother and an old woman were baking maize bread in a hole in the wall of the tomb. They had kneaded it in a wheelbarrow, and the children looked as if they needed it, too. *Bono joko!*

On our way back, when nearly as far as the old walls, we turned down a lane to visit the catacombs of Calixtus. Candles were provided, and we went down to the second tier; there are five of these, one below another. I do not know how far we went, but it seemed miles—passages just wide enough for me to pass through, opening into rooms every now and then, and with many cross-roads where one could soon be lost. Here were countless graves, here and there skeletons, emblems, places for lamps, frescoes of ancient date, and many interesting memorials. It was a new scene to me, but deeply solemn and touching. Think of it,—that this was only one set of chambers and passages, and that there was one above, and three deeper down! There are from five to six graves, one above the other, in each passage, and the whole place is full right along. These tombs are open in most cases, for the doors or stones which closed them are taken away to museums. This is the best and most convenient catacomb for tourists to see; but there are, I believe, sixty others. They have no Popery in them, and I would sooner live and die in them than live in this city of Babylon. It is nothing less than what the Bible calls it; it is full of idols, filthy rag, bone, and rubbish worship of the most abominable kind. I have cursed it all, as Paul did those who preach "another gospel."

Then we drove to St. John Lateran, "the mother of all churches," and I shall here only dare to write of one thing which, to my dying day, I shall never forget. I do not know that I ever felt my blood boil so with indignation or my heart melt so much with pity as when I saw the Santa Scala, down which our blessed Lord is said to have come from Pilate's hall. It was a pitiable sight to see old people, grey-headed men, young women, and little children with their mothers, crawling up and down this staircase on their knees, kissing the bottom step, and touching it with their forehead, and doing likewise to the middle and top steps, because they say our Savior fainted at those places.

SANTA SCALA, ROME

As I stood there, I could only pray that another Luther might arise, and thunder forth the fact that men are not justified by works, but by faith alone. It was an awful thought to me that all these poor creatures should believe that they gained a hundred days' indulgence and the pardon of their sins every time they crawled up that staircase, and that every stop their knees kneeled on meant so many days less of purgatory for them. The stairs are covered with wood, which has been three times renewed, having been worn away by the knees of the votaries! My heart feels all on a blaze with righteous anger. O miserable, world, thus to dishonor the ever-blessed Lamb! O infinite mercy, which permits such insulters to live! I have seen them adoring thigh-bones, skulls, arms, and hands—yes, actually *adoring* these things as if they were Divine! Pagan Rome never went this length.

We went to St. Peter's to finish the day with music, and it was fine indeed; but I was jostled in a crowd of people so highly perfumed with garlic, that I soon made my escape to the outskirts to have another look round the great joss-house. Here I learned some English history, for I saw Canova's tomb to the memory of James III., Charles III., and Henry IX., Kings of England! Ask the boys if they ever read of them. They were the last of the Stuarts—the Pretender,—his son, Charles Edward, or "bonnie Prince Charlie,"—and his son. What hundreds of other things I have seen this day, cannot now, and perhaps never will be told. I have stayed up late to put this down for fear of forgetting it, and also because it may be I shall have less time tomorrow when preparing to preach. God bless thee, dearest, and be thou glad, with me, that no "strong delusion to believe a lie" has fallen upon us. Today has taught me a year's learning. The Lord make it useful to His Church!

I send a picture of the Pope's coachman. What a swell he is! I think you will like the portrait of a brigand's wife. It is very well executed, and if you like it too much to part with it, be sure to keep it. The fellow in red is awful; these *confratelli* are in all colors according to the degree, of the buried person. They are good fellows, who bury the dead *"pour l'amour de Dieu,"* and they belong to all ranks in Rome. They cover themselves up in this manner to avoid recognition, and escape praise. They are universally respected, but look horribly ugly. I think they will make a sensation in the magic-lantern.

Yesterday morning, when I preached in the Presbyterian Chapel, all was quiet and delightful; but at night, in Rome, while, my words were being translated by Mr. Wall, we were stopped by questioners. It was requested that they would reserve their inquiries till the end of the service, but the opponents were impatient. A paper was passed up from a Catholic lady, to say that a secular priest was present, a man of great ability, and a personal friend of the Pope, and that he was sent on purpose to discuss. So, presently, a man of unprepossessing appearance began to assail us with arguments from a skeptical standpoint, upon which he received such an answer that he shifted his ground, and declared that none had any right to teach save "the Church." Mr. Wall replied to this, and the man changed his tactics again. Then, up rose a Waldensian minister, who spoke so well that the people broke out in cheers and clapping. This was suppressed, and again the enemy thundered forth his threats. He was answered by several, and told that he had shifted his ground, and was a priest; and Mr. Wall challenged him to a public dispute at any place he chose to name. This he declined, and seeing that the people grew warm, he wisely withdrew. One word from us, and he would have been put out of the window. The incident pleased Mr. Wall, for it created excitement, and will bring more to hear; but I was far from happy about it, and would gladly have been spared such a scene. Glory be to God, there is a living church in Rome, and the way in which they have gained converts has been by opposition; the notoriety which it has given them has brought many to hear the gospel. Bravely the work goes on, and the baptized lead the way. The leaders are two good fellows, pronounced Baptists, believing firmly that their church is that of the catacombs, and the only true Church of Christ in Rome; the others, they say, are the churches of Luther, and Knox, and Wesley, and Waldo,—theirs is the only old original. I gently combat their restrictiveness, but do not wonder at it.

BAPTISTERY IN CATACOMB OF ST. PONZIANO, ROME.

We have been to another catacomb, one not often visited. It is named after St. Ponziano, and is situated outside Rome, in a vineyard, a good way from the walls, and though truly ancient, it is not very far opened up, but you have to go down very deep. A man, who calls himself "the dove of the catacombs" (he must mean "bat "), took us down. We went a long, long way, each of us carrying a taper, and at last we came to a place, where some eight roads meet underground. Seven of these were closed, but we found what we had specially come to see. This was a baptistery. It was full of sweet, clear, running water, about four feet deep, and above it was a painting in fresco of our Lord standing up to his waist in the water, and John putting his hand on the sacred head, that it, too, might be immersed; he was not *pouring* the water on him. Here we stood, and prayed to the blessed One into whose Name we had been buried by baptism. It was a solemn moment. Here also were two other frescoes of our Lord,—very beautiful faces; and the Alpha and Omega, and Christian monogram symbols, which are so plain and natural that they do not come under the head of superstition. There were, however, bones in plenty, and the place was very hot and close, so we were glad soon to escape into the open air, for even holy dust is not the best purifier, or the best provender for living lungs.

A COLUMBARIUM, ROME.

You would have liked to have been with us when we went to see the *columbaria,* near the St. Sebastian gate. We visited two of them; they are singular places, like vast dovecots, but they are not for doves. It is strange to look upon the spot where thousands upon thousands of Rome's wealthy citizens have for many ages lain in little heaps of ashes. The bodies, of the dead were burned, and the dust was preserved in small urns which were kept in these curious places. Some persons had a family *columbarium;* in other cases, companies were formed for their construction, and they were then let out in portions as required. The niches are like small vaulted chambers, and there will be in them, sometimes an urn, some-times a lamp, or a small bust, while frequently the name and age of the deceased will be found on a slab of marble over the recess. In each of these small spaces, there are two holes sunk to receive the ashes if an urn is not used, and these have lids to cover the remains. These great square buildings contained many hundreds of these "nests" for the dead, and a visit to them leaves a strangely-solemn impression on the mind.

I had two such precious letters from you this morning, worth to me far more than all the gems of ancient or modern art. The material of which they are composed is their main value, though there is also no mean skill revealed in its manipulation. They are pure as alabaster, far more precious than porphyry or verd antique;

no mention shall be made of malachite or onyx, for love surpasses them all.

We are off to Naples today.

Chapter 74

THE BAY OF NAPLES.—PAINTED BY DR. JOBSON, AND PRESENTED BY HIM TO MR. SPURGEON, "IN REMEMBRANCE OF TRAVEL TOGETHER IN ITALY."

THIS MORNING, we drove through Naples for, I should think, six or seven miles or more. It is a crowded city, full of stirs, full of business, and full of pleasure. Horses seem innumerable, they are decorated profusely, and the carriages are very comfortable; but, I am sorry to say, the men drive furiously, and make me very nervous. Old women are numerous and hideous, beggars pestiferous, and dealers intensely persevering. But what a bay! What a sea and climate! No one ought to be ill here.

We have been over the museum,—full of frescoes from Pompeii, gleanings from the catacombs, pickings from the Appian Way, stealings from the baths of Caracalla and other places. Naples has taken away from Rome the best of the ancient statuary and treasures, and prepared a vast museum for the spoils. We saw thousands of precious things, enough for a year's inspection; but the Pompeian remains were the most important. There were surgical instruments exactly like those of the present day;—cottage-loaves of bread, stewpans, colanders, ladles, and all cookery things just like our own. The safes for money were just like old plate-Chests. There were cotton, silk, and thread, in skeins and hanks, and large knitting and netting needles. Indeed, the people then had all we have now; even earthen money-boxes with a slit in the top, such as the children have in our country villages. There were plenty of proofs that the people were sinners, and of a scarlet dye, too. It was curious to see the colors in a painter's shop, the bottles and drugs of a Chemist, and the tools of other traders. We saw also a splendid collection of ancient gems and cameos, most costly and lovely. I never saw so many gathered together before.

We drove from the museum to the site of a new field of lava, which flowed down from Vesuvius last April. It is just beyond the houses of suburban Naples, and was very different from what I had expected. It had crossed our road, and passed on through a vineyard,—this was one tongue of the stream. Then we crossed a second by a road made near it, and came to a village through which the largest stream had burned its way. It is a huge incandescent sea of the outflow of the volcano men were blasting and using pickaxes to open up the road which the flood had completely blocked. We were soon upon the lava; it has a surface like a heap of ashes, supposing that every ash should weigh a ton or two. It is still hot, and in some places smoking. I should have investigated it carefully, and with interest, only a horde of children, beggars, and women with babies gave us no rest, but continued crying, and imploring alms, and offering us pieces picked out of the mass. Much of the strange material is far too hot to hold, and our feet felt the heat as we walked across the surface. The stream has partly destroyed several houses, and cut the village in two; people are living in the half of a house which stands, the other half being' burned and filled up with the molten substance. Vesuvius, high above us, is only giving out a little smoke, and seems quiet enough. As I could never climb up to the crater, I think we shall be content to have seen this lava torrent.

Our hotel here is vast and empty; we have excellent rooms, and are thoroughly comfortable. There is music continually, and very fair music, too, though not so sweet as silence. Everybody makes all the noise possible, and quiet dwells beyond the sea. Rome is a sepulcher, this city teems with life. You are not out of the door a moment before you are entreated to have a carriage, buy fruit, fish, pictures, papers, or something. The side-streets swarm with people, who appear to live in them; there they eat, cook, work, catch fleas;, hunt over each other's heads like so many monkeys, etc., etc. It is like living in a museum; but as to the beauty and gracefulness of which we read so much, I cannot detect it, though really looking for it. Persons over forty look worn out, and females at that age are haggard; over that period, they are. ghastly and mummified. Macaroni hangs out, in some quarters, before the doors on lines to dry; and the flies, which are numerous upon it, give it anything but an attractive appearance. Tomorrow, we hope to go to Pompeii. I am now thinking about next month's Magazine, and devoutly wish I could light upon a subject for an article,—but my brain is dull.

We have seen Pompeii. We drove there, and it took us three hours, almost all of it between long lines of houses, like one continuous street. At the town of Resina, we passed Herculaneum, but did not enter it, as Pompeii is more worth seeing. Then we went through a town which has, I think, been seven times destroyed by Vesuvius, and is now crowded with people. There we saw the lava by the side of, and under the houses, hard as a rock; and the roads are generally paved with great flags of the same material. Though driving by the shore of the bay, we seldom saw the water, for even where there was no town, there were high walls, and, worst of all, off the stones the white dust was suffocating, and made us all look like millers. However, we reached Pompeii at last, and I can only say, in a sentence, it exceeds in interest all I have seen before, even in Rome. I walked on, on, on, from twelve to four o'clock, lost in wonder amid the miles of streets of this buried city, now silent and open to the gazer's eye. To convey a worthy idea of it to you, would be impossible, even in a ream of paper.

We entered at the Street of Tombs, which was outside the gate. In it were houses, shops, taverns, a fountain, and several tombs. The house of Diomed greatly interested us. We went upstairs and downstairs, and then into the cellars where were still the amphorae, or wine-bottles, leaning against the wall in rows, the pointed end being stuck into the ground, and the rows set together in dry dust, in exactly the same way as we place articles in sawdust. In the cellars were found eighteen skeletons of women who had fled there for shelter.

THE HOUSE AND GARDEN OF DIOMED, POMPEII

The photograph I send shows the garden, with covered walk round it, and tank for live fish. In this street were several places for seats in the shade, made in. great semicircles, so that a score of persons could rest at once. Near the gate was the niche where the soldier was found who kept his watch while others fled. We could not think of going up and down all the streets; it would need many days to see all. The city was, I should think, a watering-place for the wealthy. No poor class of houses has yet been discovered. It was paved with great slabs, of stone, which are worn deeply with cart or chariot wheels. Across the streets were huge stepping-stones, just wide enough to allow wheels to go on each side; but either they had no horses to the cars in these streets, or else they must have been trained to step over. In some places were horsing-blocks, in others; there were holes in the kerbstone to pass a rope through to tie up a horse. The houses are many of theta palaces, and contained great treasures of art, which are now in museums, but enough is left in each case to show what they were. Frescoes remain in abundance, and grottoes, and garden fountains, and marble terraces for cascades of water. It is a world of wonders.

In one part of the city, a noble owner had let the corner of his house to a vendor of warm wines, and there, is his marble counter, with the holes therein for his warming-pots. Stains of wine were on the counter when it was first uncovered.

THE HOUSE OF SALLUST, POMPEII.

We saw the back parlor of a drinking-shop, with pictures on the wall of a decidedly non-teetotal character. There were several bakers' shops with hand-mills, the tops of which turned round on a stone, and ground well, no doubt. In one, we saw the oven, with a water-jar near it,—in this place were found 183 loaves of bread.

In the doctors' and chemists' shops, when opened, they saw the medicines as they were when entombed, and even pills left in the process of rolling! In the custom-house were standard weights and measures. Soap factories have their evaporating-pans remaining. Oil vessels abound; and in one, made of glass, some of the oil may still be seen. Cookshops had in them all the stewpans, gridirons, and other necessities of the trade. We saw jewelers' shops, artists' studios, and streets of grocers' and drapers' shops, many with signs over their doors. The baths impressed me much, to they had been newly built when the awful tragedy took place, and look as if they were opened yesterday;—a fine cold plunge-bath, with water carried high for a "shower", a dressing-room with niches for brushes, combs, and pomades,—all of which were there, but have been removed to museums;—and a great brazier in green bronze, with seats round it for the bathers to dry themselves;—a warm bath, and a vapor bath all perfect, and looking ready for use tomorrow.

The Forum was vast, and had in it the facades of several magnificent temples, the remains of which reveal their former glory. The pedestals of the statues of the eminent men of the town remain with their names upon them. We saw the tragic and comic theatres, and the amphitheater which held 20,000 persons, in which the people were assembled when the eruption came, and from which they escaped, but had to flee to the fields, and leave their houses for ever.

THE AMPHITHEATRE, POMPEII.

In the Temple of Isis, we saw the places where the priests were concealed when they made the goddess deliver her oracles! We saw the lady herself in the museum, with a pipe at the back of her head, which was fixed in the wall, and served as, the secret speaking-tube. The priests of His were found dead at her shrine; one of them with an axe had cut through two walls to get out, but had not succeeded. Poor creature!

THE FORUM, POMPEII.

171

In a money-changer's house, we saw his skeleton, lying on its face, with outstretched arms and hands much money was found near him. In the barracks were sixty-three persons, soldiers' and officers' wives. Here were the stocks which had been used for the punishment of refractory soldiers.

THE STREET OF MERCURY, POMPEII.

In the Street of Mercury is a triumphal arch, on which stood a statue of Nero, found nearly perfect. Here, too, we noted a drinking-fountain, and a house with its exterior richly adorned with red frescoes. In a vast Hall of Justice were cells under the magistrates' bench; and in these, three prisoners were found, inside an iron ring which went round their waists. They were, perhaps, waiting to be brought up before the aldermen for some misdemeanor, and expecting to be fined "five shillings and costs," but they perished like their betters, and were summoned before a higher tribunal.

Out of so great a city, I suppose comparatively few were destroyed; so, as the bodies of these are found, they are preserved, especially if anything remarkable is to be seen in connection with them.

We saw the digging still going on, and the mounds of removed, rubbish were like high railway embankments. No roofs remain, but spouts for the rain-water are there in great abundance; they are in the. form of dogs' and lions' heads and other quaint devices. No stables have yet been uncovered; but the carts, which stood at the inn doors, have left their iron tires, the skeletons of the horses, and their bits, to bear witness to their former existence. Skeletons of dogs and cats were there, and in a pan was a sucking pig prepared and just ready for roasting! I saw also a pot on a tripod, or trivet, which, when discovered, actually had water in it! I feel ashamed to write so badly on such a theme, but I cannot do better. It is too vast a task for me, and I fail to recollect a tithe of it. I must cease writing tonight, but I continue to breathe loving assurances to my sweet wifey.

We have been in a steamer to the Island of Capri, calling at Sorrento on the way;—a glorious excursion, but we failed in our great object, which was, to see the Blue Grotto. The sea was too rough to permit entrance, as the opening is only three feet high, and no one can get in except during smooth water, and when the wind is from a certain quarter. However, vie stayed a couple of hours on the island, which is precipitous, so I did not climb, but sat on a balcony, enjoying the marvelous, scene. We reached Naples late, for the boat was slow; but first the sunset, and then the moonlight, gave us two charming effects, to which Vesuvius added by booking almost continuously. This little trip served as a pleasant rest and refreshment after the toil and the dust of Pompeii.

Today, we have had a long and splendid drive to the other side of the bay. First along the quay, then through a tunnel almost half a mile long, and then skirting the bay, by road to Puteoli, where Paul landed;—we saw the spot (as is supposed), and the commencement of the Appian Way which he followed till he reached Rome. At Puteoli, we first went into the crater of the Solfatara, a semi-extinct volcano, which has not been in eruption since 1198, when it destroyed ancient Puteoli. It is grown over with shrubs and small trees. A man throws down a big stone, which makes it all sound, and shows you that the whole vast area is hollow. You are fed to a great hole in the side of the hill, whence pours out, with the roar of an engine blowing off steam, a great quantity of sulphureous vapor. All around is; brimstone, and with a long kind of hoe a man rakes out bits from the mouth of the huge oven. The ground is very hot, and an odor, which is anything but dainty, prevails. You can go right up to it with perfect ease and safety. The vapor is; said to cure gout, but one must stand in it some time every day for a month! When Vesuvius is Furious, Solfatara subside so there seems good evidence that the two, though twelve miles apart, are vents of the same fires. We looked down on the Temple of Serapis; it has been up and down, and in and out of the sea several times, as; the restless coast hats risen or fallen. It is now out of water, but is remarkable rather for its history than for its present beauty.

We drove on by the crater Of Monte Barbaro and that of Monte Nuovo. This last volcano sprang up in a night in 1538, covered a village, stopped a great canal, and did no end of mischief; but since then it has been quiet, and allowed itself to furnish soil enough for brushwood, which makes it look like a green pyramid. On the other side of this hill is the famous lake of Avernus, of which Virgil wrote, and by the side of which he placed the entrance to Hades. The dense woods which smothered it have been cut down, and it has by no means a repulsive appearance now; but it is a channel for the escape of noxious gases, and is, no doubt, the crater of a volcano. We did not enter the Sybil's Cave, or otherwise inquire of Pluto and Proserpine; but drove on, through the ruined city of Cumae, to the lake of Fusaro or Acheron, another circular basin. Here oysters were cultivated till the lake gave out mephitic vapors, and killed the bivalves. The water has become pure again, and the industry has recommenced. Passing by Virgil's Elysian fields, and manifold wonders, we came to Misenum, and the village of Bacoli. Here we left the carriage, and ascended the hill to see what is called the Piscina Mirabilis,—a vast underground reservoir, which once contained water brought by the Julian aqueduct from some fifty miles' distance. It is dry now, and we descended a long flight of steps to the bottom. It has a roof supported by forty-eight huge columns; it is 220 feet long, and 82 feet broad. There are traces of water having filled it up to the spring of the arches, and the place where the water entered is very plainly to be seen. There are great openings in the root; down which hang festoons of creeping plants. The place was very chilly, and coming up forty steps out of it seemed like leaving a sepulcher. Yet it was a sight to be remembered to one's dying day. We descended through the foul and loathsome village street, where cholera may well rage in summer. We could not explore villas of Julius Caesar, prisons of Nero, villa of Agrippina, and other places, for we were tired, and I felt afraid of more vaults and their horrible damps. So we went-into Baiae, and entered a queer little *osteria,* or inn, and had some poor would-be oysters, bread and butter, and green lemons, freshly gathered from the tree. The view was glorious indeed, nothing could excel it; great ruined temples and villas were everywhere, and made a picture of exceeding beauty.

The drive home was by the sea, and we could perceive buildings down at the bottom, under the clear blue water. These have been brought down by the depression of the land upon which they stood, owing to earthquakes. We crossed a lava torrent which had come from Monte Nuova, and then we went on by our former road though Puteoli, till we left it to return to Naples without traversing the tunnel. This road took us up on one side of the promontory of Posilippo, whence we saw Ischia, Puteoli, Baize, and Misenum; and then we went down the other side, with Capri, Sorrento, Vesuvius, and Naples, all in full view. We were quickly down among the grand equipages which fill the Riviera di Chiaia; and, dashing along as fast as any of them, we were soon at the hotel door; and, since *table d'hôte,* I have been writing this long narration for you. The air here is balmy, the atmosphere dry, the heat great in the sun, but bearable in the shade. Mosquitoes are fewer and less voracious than in Venice. Everything is restorative to the system, and exhilarating. Even the beggars seem to be happy. None are miserable but the old women and the priests. Organs are far too plentiful, and music of all sorts is *ad nauseam.* Of religion, I have only seen one trace, namely, the towing down of everyone when "the host" was being carried under an umbrella to some sick person, Beggar's swarm, and dealers in little wares assail you at all points, and will not cease their importunities, Tomorrow will be the Sabbath, and in this I rejoice, for rest is sweet, and sweetest when made "holiness to the Lord." I send tons of love to you, hot as fresh lava. God bless you with His best blessings!

PANORAMA OF NAPLES.

It is the Sabbath, quiet and restful. We have had a delightful service, and I have written for my note-book and the Magazine; so there will be a little less for my dear one, but there is nothing new to tell. I have been so grandly well all this time that I do not know how to be grateful enough, and my heart is light because you are better; my soul is at rest, my spirit leaps. I am indeed a debtor to Him who restoreth my soul. Blessed be His holy Name for ever and ever! We are very quiet, for there are no other visitors in the house; we have the best rooms, nice beds, well-curtained from mosquitoes. There is a house between us and the sea, but we can see the bay on each side of it, and Vesuvius if we go out on the balcony. The climate is like Heaven below, and cannot but be a medicine to the sick. I send you a photograph of a slave who was found in Pompeii close behind his master, and carrying a bag of money, both of them endeavoring to escape. It is a perfect model, covered with incrustations.

I have also sent the photograph of a grotto, or rather, ancient fountain in mosaic, which is in one of the houses.

They used to put a lamp inside the grotesque heads. Water fell in a little cascade down the steps. It seems in odd taste, but there are several such in the gardens of the buried villas.

Tomorrow we hope to be travelling; God be with thee, mine own, and give thee peace and healing! My heart is everywhere and ever thine.

ANCIENT FOUNTAIN, POMPEII.

Again in Rome. Waking somewhat early this morning, I have risen to write to mine own darling wife. The fact is, I am afraid there will be a gap in the correspondence, and I shall be very sorry if it turns out to be so. Just as we left Naples, the rain began to descend, the warmth was gone, and we had a cool, if not a cold journey here. The fall in the temperature seemed to affect me, and I had a very disturbed and uncomfortable night. I am, however, so grateful for my long spell of rest, night by night, that this does not depress me, although I hoped that I was getting beyond the reach of such restless hours.

Yesterday was wet every now and then, but I had to devote the day to the Magazine, and therefore it mattered not. I stole out to the Pantheon, and the Lateran, and then again. Not being in harness, I worked slowly, and the matter came not until the mind had been much squeezed! How much more pleasant is the outbursting juice of the grape when it yields its streams to the lightest pressure of the vintner's hand! Yet duty had to be done, and I did it; but have more yet to do. Three dear letters awaited me here. "Not worth sixpence," did you say? They are worth a mint to me; they are mosaics of which every little bit is at Fern. Naples has been a great treat; how I wish you could have been there, but I Should not like you to see how horses are treated, it would make you quite unhappy. The Neapolitans load up their carriages most cruelly. I never saw so many horses, mules, and donkeys in my life before in proportion to the people. Everybody drives or rides, and they are all in a great hurry, too. Now, my hand, this brings great galleons of love to you, and a cargo of kisses lie,; under the hatches. Just pull them up, and let the creatures fly in the air; innumerable they will be as the clouds of doves which flew over the olive gardens of Judaea in the olden time, and every one has its own tender voice. God give thee still thy daily patience while He sees fit to send thee pain; but, oh! may He remove the affliction, and send healing to thee, and brighter days to us both! Nevertheless, His will be done!

Florence.—By an unfortunate mistake as to train, we were prevented from leaving Rome early this morning, so we have done a little more sight-seeing. One of our party is of the Mark Tapley school, and always persuades us that any hitch in our plans is a capital thing, and could not have happened better. We went off to Santa Maria Maggiore, and there saw the various chapels, and precious stones, and rare marbles, and bronzes, etc., etc. The old verger was so eloquent, in Italian that I made out nearly all he said. Then we went to the Borghese Palace, and saw long rooms of pictures, mostly saints and virgins. In these rooms were two sweet little fountains of water, and glasses; for the visitors to drink from. This is a private palace, but the public are always welcome. Then we found our way to the Jesuits' Church, where there was uncovered a silver statue of Loyola, of price, less value for the gems set in it, and the masses of *lapis lazuli*. Afterwards, we sat on the Pincian till the rain came, and it has poured down ever since, making our journey to this place a more weary one than usual. Everything is shrouded in mist, mildewed and funereal, except the young waterfalls, which leap like lions' whelps from Bashan, and laugh, and fling themselves about in their glee.

Genoa.—We left Florence on Friday, and the day was fine, so that we greatly enjoyed the journey over the mountains to Bologna. Then it is a dull road to Alessandria, which we reached about six o'clock. Thence to Genoa should take two hours and a-half; but, in ascending the Maritime Alps, there was snow, and the engine crawled along, and at last stopped altogether. Think of it,—going up hill, and stopping! The steam was put on, and the wheels revolved, sending out a shower of sparks, but the train did not stir. Then came men with spades to clear away some snow, and after a while the carriages moved, we gained the top of the hill, and ran down all right, getting into Genoa about 10 p.m. A long, tiresome day.

Here, where we were so comfortable last year, we were marched up four sets of stairs, and then shown into rooms which had a most offensive smell. The house was full, the waiter said, and they could give us no other rooms. We replied, "Very well, then, we will go somewhere else;" and when we had carried all our luggage to the door, apartments were found for us on the first floor!

This morning, expecting to leave for Mentone at twelve o'clock, we hear that the line is broken in four places, and no train goes except at eight am., so we are here till Monday. It rains, and has rained all night in torrents. We must wait, and then go on in great uncertainty and sure discomfort. Never mind! it will serve me for illustration, no doubt. Dr. Jobson, a Wesleyan minister, has had an hour's happy chat with me, and very much interested me. He is a holy, liberal-hearted soul, and we enjoy a conversation together, so it is not all dullness. It is beginning to clear up while I am writing, so perhaps we may get a walk. I have had restful nights this week, and. am still really much better, but the damp and cold try me a good deal.

Sabbath.—This day, which we have been forced to spend here, has not been an unhappy one, but a sweet day, most calm and bright. The rain cleared off yesterday about four o'clock, enabling us to wander through the narrow streets of Genoa la Superba, and to enter several of the churches. My indignation was stirred beyond measure when, upon looking into the confessional boxes,[1] I read the directions to the priest as to the questions he should ask the penitents. These were printed in Latin, and referred to those unmentionable crimes which brought fire upon Sodom, and are the curse of heathendom. To see young maidens kneel down to be asked such questions as these, made me wish that every priest could be cut off from the face of the earth as unfit to live, and I most deliberately invoked upon them all the righteous vengeance of an insulted God! Since I came away, my more sober reflections fully endorse my indignant wrath. How can the Lord endure all this? Truly, His patience is great.

Today we had our breaking of bread, and Dr. Jobson and his wife joined us. The good old man spoke most sweetly, and prayed for you with great pathos, and much faith that the Lord would yet heal you. He shamed me by his faith, and I blessed him for his tender affection. The Lord was with us, and the season will be memorable to us all. Then I revised a sermon, which is not quite finished yet; but the *table d'hôte* bell is ringing, so I must needs pause a while, and allow the body to feed in its turn. Today is; fine and bright, and has been warm in the sun. We have large leads to walk on, and I have had a little turn there while the others have gone up on the heights for a walk. Tomorrow, I hope, will be equally clear, and then we shall not mind the getting out and in where the railway is broken.

Table d'hôte is now over, and I have had the old Doctor in for a talk, though I wanted to be alone, and go on with my sermon and letters. However, the good soul is gone now, and I can get to my dear work of communing with my darling by the pen. Every memory of you is full of joy, except your illness; and that makes me love you all the more, by adding sympathy. I am afraid I am still a rough, forgetful being, so apt to get absorbed in my work, and to think too little of you; but this is not in my heart, but is in my nature; and I suppose, if it were not there, I could not do my work so successfully. You know and love me too well to judge as others would. We have to be off early in the morning, so I must close this note.

Mentone.—We came here yesterday from Genoa, and a very interesting journey it was. We left Genoa at eight o'clock, and went on all right till ten, when we all had to get out, for the road was destroyed. We walked down a lane, then over a bridge, then down on. the other side, and up the embankment, and got into another train. In this case, the bridge of the railway was broken by a torrent, and a break indeed it was. In due time, we went on; but, in an hour or so, came to a dead halt, and had to get out again. This time the walk was long, and the way went through a vineyard, and up a steep bank. Crowds of men and boys clamored for our luggage, and followed us all the half-mile we had to trudge. We had to wait forty minutes till another train came; and then, when We scrambled in, they quietly shoved us out of the way, and made us sit still for forty minutes more. We went on at little, only to stop again; and, at last, at Porto Maurizio, we had the carriages pushed by men over a dangerous place, and then hooked on to another train. However, we reached Ventimiglia safely at about seven o'clock, and then had an hour to wait to have dinner. We left there at 8 p.m., and arrived here at 7:20 p.m., this last being the greatest feat I ever performed! To travel for twenty minutes, and then to lind the clock forty minutes behind the time at which you started, is a gain not to be despised;—the explanation is that Roman time is used at Ventimiglia, and Paris time at Mentone. The day was fine, and though the way was long, the adventures made the hours pass away merrily, and our Mark Tapley friend was quite in his element. We are at a most comfortable hotel, and everyone tries to please us. The landlord knew me at once, and shook hands heartily, saying, "How do you do, reverend? I am very glad to see you!"

Today, while I was lying on the beach, and. Mark Tapley was slyly filling our pockets with stones, and rolling Mr. Passmore over, who should walk up but Mr. McLaren, of Manchester, with whom I had a long and pleasant chat. We are to go to Monaco tomorrow together. He has three months' holiday. I am glad I have not; but I should wish I had, if I had my dear wife with me to enjoy it. Poor little soul! she must suffer while I ramble. Two clergymen have had a long talk with me this evening. It began by one saying aloud to the other, "I hear Mr. Spurgeon has been here." This caused a titter round the table, for I was sitting opposite to him. Mentone is charming, but not very warm. It is as I like it, and is calculated to make a sick man leap with health. How I wish you could be here!

We have had another day here of the sweetest rest. We drove to Monaco and back, and saw to perfection the little rocky Principality. Its lovely gardens and promenades are kept up by the profits of the gaming-tables, which are in a far more sumptuous palace than those at Baden-Baden, which we saw together years ago. We had Mr. McLaren with us and went in and watched the players. One gentleman monopolized our attention; he was a fine-looking Englishman, like an officer. He lost a pile of money, and went out apparently most wretched and excited. Soon, he came in again, and changed bills for 3,000 francs, and began playing heavily. He won, and got back his bills; and when we left, we saw him come out; I could only hope that God had delivered him, and that he would be wise, and never go to the table, again. It is a vortex which sucks in a vast number of Victims day by day. What moths men are if the candle be but bright enough!

The two parsons here are High Church and Low Church, and I have had a talk with both. Just before dinner, who should go by but the Earl of Shaftesbury, with whom I had half-an-hour's converse. He was very low in spirit, and talked as if all things in the world were going wrong; but I reminded him that our God was yet alive, and that dark days were only the signs of better times coming. He is a real nobleman; and man of God. Everybody in the hotel is courteous and kind, and I have quite a circle of acquaintances already. I have enjoyed the rest very much; but young married couples remind me of our early days, and the cloud which covers us now. Still, He who sent both sun and shade is our ever-tender Father, and knows best; and if it be good for us, He can restore all that He has withdrawn, and more; and if not, He designs our yet greater good. There is nothing more to write, except the ever true and never tiresome message,—my perfect love be with thee, and the Lord's love be over thee for ever! In a few more days I shall see thee, and it will be a fairer sight than any my eyes have rested on during my absence.

Yesterday, Mr. and Mrs. in tiller went with me to Dr. Bennet's garden, and I had a most profitable conversation with him, one to be remembered for many a day with delight. Dr. Bennet came up, and I was amused to hear Muller teaching him the power of prayer, and recommending him to pray about one of the terraces which he wants to buy, but the owner asks a hundred times its value. Dr. B. thought it too trifling a matter to take to the Lord; he said that Mr. Muller might very properly pray about the Orphanage, but as to this terrace, to complete his garden,—he thought he could not make out a good case about it. Mr. M. said it encouraged people in sin if we yielded to covetous demands, so he thought the Dr. might pray that the owners should be kept from exorbitant claims; but Dr. B. said that, as ignorant peasants, they were very excusable for trying either to keep their land, or to get all they could from an Englishman whom they imagined to be a living gold mine! The spirit of both was good; but, of course, the simple, child-like holy trust of Muller was overpowering. He is not a sanctimonious person; but full of real joy, and sweet peace, and innocent pleasure.

Nice.—In this; place we have been put up four flights of stairs, and, alas! into very cold rooms. I woke in the night, and felt as, it I were freezing in a vault, and my ankles were in great pain. I was much cast down; and, on getting out of bed, found the carpet and floor both very damp. I had a very bad night, and am now in much pain in the left foot. Yet I believe I shall get over it soon, and

I mean to have no more of these climbings up stairs, and sleeping in horrid cells. Nice is a very grand place, and I am sorry we left Mentone to come to it. But I must not write in a grumbling vein. Here have I had nearly five weeks of good health, and have grown stronger every day; why should I care for one little relapse? We will be off to Cannes and Hyeres, and. see what God has in store for us. He will deal graciously with me as He has ever done.

Cannes.—I was too ill yesterday to write. After the deadly chili of Thursday night at Nice, I felt the gout coming on, but resolved to escape from that inhospitable hotel. An hour brought us here, but it rained mercilessly, and all around was damp and chill. I got upstairs into beautiful rooms, but had to go to bed, which I have only left for a moment or two since, while it was being arranged. My left foot is badly swollen, and the knee-joint is following suit. I have had very little sleep, and am very low; but, oh, the kindness of these friends! They sit up with me all night by turns, and cheer me with promises. I hope I shall get home in time for Sunday, but have some fears of it. Do not fret about me, I may be well before this reaches you; and if I am, I will telegraph and say so. I have every comfort here but home, and my dear wifey's sweet words. I am sad that my journey should end so, but the Lord's will be done!

Two days later.—I have had a heavy time of pain, my dearest, but am now better. God has changed the weather;—yesterday was warm, today is hot, so we think it best to hurry on, and, if possible, have a *coupé-lit* right through to Paris. I feel well in myself, but the knee will not bear me, though I think I should be as strong as a horse after a day or two of this weather. How much I have to thank the Lord for! Such kind friends! They have proved their love beyond all praise. I was never alone. Even the *femme de chambre* pitied *"pauvre monsieur,"* and did her best for me. I hope now to get home in time for Sunday. My soul loves you, and longs to see you.

Paris.—In the hope that one more letter may reach you before I come personally, I give myself the delight of writing it. The telegram will have told you that, at the very prudent advice of the doctor, I left Cannes at 3.15 on Tuesday in a *coupé-lit* to travel direct to Paris. It has proved a very wise step. A lady lent her Bath-chair to take me to the station, and porters lifted me into the carriage. There I had a nice sofa-bed and every convenience. I lay there with great comfort till we reached Marseilles; then came the night, and

I had hoped to sleep, but the extreme oscillation of the train quite prevented that. Once only I dozed for a few minutes, yet I was kept restful till six o'clock, when my dear friends got me some warm soup, and I had a refreshing wash. Then, all day long, I was at peace till 6 p.m. From Lyons, the country is flooded all along the road; we seemed to ride through a vast river. I naturally felt the chill of this, and my knees complained. Near Paris it rained hard, and at Paris heavily. After much stress and difficulty, I was put into a cab, and we drove to this hotel. I went to bed immediately, and slept on, on, on, till eight o'clock the next morning, awaking then refreshed, and, happily, none the. worse for the long journey. I meant to stay in bed all day, and sent my friends out, so that I might not always be a drag upon them; but, at about noon, I rose and dressed, and when they came in, I had flown,—to a sitting-room and a sofa by a cozy fire! I can walk now a little, and hope to be all right for Sunday. Bless the Lord, O my soul; and may He bless thee, too, my dear heart of love! I hope to have a *coupe,* and tomorrow lie down again while travelling, and so home to my tender wifely. Who could hope to escape rheumatic pains when all the world is wet through to the center? It must not grieve you that I suffer, but you must rejoice that I escaped so long. Why, even rocks might feel this marvelous, long-continued wetting! I am indeed grateful to God for His goodness; still, "there's no place like home." This brings great loads of love all flaming. God bless thee ever!

Carriage at Victoria at 5.45, Friday!

* * * * *

NOTES

1   Spurgeon always considered the Catholic confessional "so filthy a business that no decent person could write the whole of what he knows about it." He recounted this same incident in *a book-summary* he published in 1873. He also wrote *a short article* on the subject in the May 1877 issue of *The Sword and the Trowel.*

Printed in the United States
114668LV00001B/188/P